RITES OF PASSAGE

RITES OF PASSAGE

A COMPANION TO THE YACHTING MONTHLY SERIES

Imray Laurie Norie & Wilson

Published by
Imray Laurie Norie & Wilson Ltd
Wych House The Broadway St Ives Cambridgeshire
PE27 5BT England
☎ +44 (0)1480 462114
ilnw@imray.com
www.imray.com
2020

© Text: Royal Cruising Club Pilotage Foundation 2020
© Photographs as credited
© Plans: Imray Laurie Norie & Wilson Ltd 2020

This product has been derived in part from material obtained from the UK Hydrographic Office with the permission of the UK Hydrographic Office, Her Majesty's Stationery Office.

© British Crown Copyright, 2020. All rights reserved.

Licence number GB AA - 005 - Imrays

THIS PRODUCT IS NOT TO BE USED FOR NAVIGATION

NOTICE: The UK Hydrographic Office (UKHO) and its licensors make no warranties or representations, express or implied, with respect to this product. The UKHO and its licensors have not verified the information within this product or quality assured it.

ISBN 978 178679 031 6 (Printed book)

ISBN 978 178679 052 1 (PDF book)

British Library Cataloguing in Publication Data.
A catalogue record for this title is available from the British Library.

All rights reserved. No part of this publication may be reproduced, transmitted or used in any form by any means – graphic, electronic or mechanical, including photocopying, recording, taping or information storage and retrieval systems or otherwise – without the prior permission of the Publishers.

Printed in Croatia by Denona

UPDATES AND SUPPLEMENTS

Any mid-season updates or annual supplements are published as free downloads available from www.imray.com
Printed copies are also available on request from the publishers.

FIND OUT MORE

For a wealth of further information, including passage planning guides and cruising logs for this area visit the Royal Cruising Club Pilotage Foundation website at www.rccpf.org.uk

FEEDBACK

The Royal Cruising Club Pilotage Foundation is a voluntary, charitable organisation. We welcome all feedback for updates and new information. If you notice any errors or omissions, please let us know at www.rccpf.org.uk

CAUTION

Whilst the Royal Cruising Club Pilotage Foundation, the authors and the publishers have used reasonable endeavours to ensure the accuracy of the content of this book, it contains selected information and thus is not definitive. It does not contain all known information on the subject in hand and should not be relied on alone for navigational use: it should only be used in conjunction with official hydrographical data. This is particularly relevant to the plans, which should not be used for navigation. The Pilotage Foundation, the authors and the publishers believe that the information which they have included is a useful aid to prudent navigation, but the safety of a vessel depends ultimately on the judgment of the skipper, who should assess all information, published or unpublished. The information provided in this pilot book may be out of date and may be changed or updated without notice. The Pilotage Foundation cannot accept any liability for any error, omission or failure to update such information. To the extent permitted by law, the Pilotage Foundation, the author and the publishers do not accept liability for any loss and/or damage howsoever caused that may arise from reliance on information contained in these pages.

Bearings and Lights
Any bearings are given as °T and from seaward. The characteristics of lights may be changed during the lifetime of this book. They should be checked against the latest edition of the UK Admiralty *List of Lights*.

First published as a series of abridged articles in Yachting Monthly magazine
www.yachtingmonthly.com

TRINITY HOUSE

The Royal Cruising Club Pilotage Foundation is privileged to have Trinity House as its Patron. The ongoing safety of navigation and education of mariners are common goals of both organisations.

www.trinityhouse.co.uk

Contents

Preface and acknowledgements v

1. **To the Isles of Scilly** 8
   Falmouth to New Grimsby via Mullion
   Sam Llewellyn

2. **Across Lyme Bay** 16
   Lulworth to Salcombe
   Megan Clay

3. **Across the Thames Estuary** 24
   Walton Backwaters to Ramsgate
   Peter Gibbs

4. **Across the Bristol Channel** 32
   Penzance to Milford Haven via Lundy
   Jane Cumberlidge

5. **Across the North Channel** 40
   Crinan to Rathlin Island via Plod Sgeirean
   Norman Kean

6. **Across the English Channel** 48
   Hamble to Braye
   Ros Hogbin

7. **Across the North Sea** 56
   Harwich to IJmuiden
   Garth Cooper

8. **Across the western English Channel** 64
   Falmouth to L'Aber Wrac'h
   Jason Lawrence

9. **Chenal du Four and Raz de Sein** 72
   L'Aber Wrac'h to Audierne
   Nick Chavasse

10. **Around Cape Wrath** 80
    Stromness to East Loch Tarbert
    Hugh Stewart

11. **Across the northern North Sea** 88
    Lerwick to Bergen
    Paul Heiney

12. **To St Kilda and back** 96
    Taransay to Lochmaddy via St Kilda
    Mary Max

13. **Across Biscay** 104
    Falmouth to Camariñas
    Madeleine Strobel

Index 112

ROYAL CRUISING CLUB PILOTAGE FOUNDATION

The Royal Cruising Club Pilotage Foundation was established in 1976 and is a registered charity with the charitable objective 'to advance the education of the public in the science and practice of navigation'.

The Foundation's principal activity is to collate and publish pilotage information for the benefit of cruising sailors worldwide. A team of dedicated authors and editors, all of whom are experienced sailors, work with the Foundation's publishers to update and develop its portfolio of pilot books and cruising guides.

In line with its charitable status, any surplus generated finances new publications and subsidises those publications that cover the more remote areas where commercial publication is not viable.

The Foundation's website gives full details of its activities and provides a portal for the sale or download of its books and passage planning guides, as well as Cruising Notes comprising up to date navigational and other reports.

www.rccpf.org.uk

© Martin Hatch | Dreamstime.com

Imray is the leading publisher of nautical information for leisure sailors. Combining the latest official hydrographic data with verified first-hand research, Imray charts, books and digital products present quality information to the highest standard.

Imray was formed in 1904 when three nautical publishing firms, each with a history from the mid 18th century, joined. Today, it works with well-known authors and organisations, covering popular sailing areas worldwide. It has been publishing Royal Cruising Club Pilotage Foundation books since the 1970s.

www.imray.com

How do you measure sailing experience?

For most of us it will be harbours visited and miles logged. But there's more to it than just numbers; certain stretches of water pose unique challenges and their reputations hold a strange power in the imagination of all who set sail.

Completing one of these passages is an initiation, a rite of passage, that engenders the respect of others and a new self-confidence. With a nod to the 1980s Yachting Monthly book, *Classic Passages*, we have collated a dozen or so of the milestone passages through, around and across British waters that should be on every cruising sailor's to-do list. So how many have you done?

Theo Stocker
Yachting Monthly

Preface and acknowledgements

Rites of Passage was conceived during a conversation between the Royal Cruising Club Pilotage Foundation and Yachting Monthly at a Southampton Boat Show. The hope was once again to enthuse and inspire us all to stretch our boundaries within home waters - and then a bit further afield.

Each of the following chapters was first published in Yachting Monthly during 2019. We go to print with this complete collection at a time when Covid remains rampant and the full realities of post-Brexit cruising seem uncertain. Now, more than ever, it feels timely to consider challenging ourselves with some new passages in home and adjacent waters. It's good to be reminded that a rich variety of new cruising grounds are only a passage away.

Tidal streams for each passage have been included to help with planning. For more information and further inspiration for all of the cruising areas we have also included additional 'Why visit?' sections. I also encourage you to read the cruising guides recommended at the end of each chapter. All are available via www.imray.com.

Combining the disparate styles of thirteen different authors within the remits of both publishers has been a challenge in itself, but I am very grateful to everyone involved for their enthusiasm, and patience, in bringing this collaborative project together.

It would never have got off the ground without the initial vision of Nick Charman, Royal Cruising Club Pilotage Foundation, who cajoled and shepherded to ensure delivery of all the articles and additional texts and photographs. Similarly instrumental were Theo Stocker and Katy Stickland at Yachting Monthly and Lucy Wilson at Imray, who ran with the idea and helped to develop and shape the whole. Debbie Wilson at Imray created all of the plans and Elinor Cole, Jenny Taylor-Jones and Sarah Douglas all worked on the production with their usual skill and professionalism.

Of course, our biggest thanks must go to all of the authors, named in the chapters that follow. They have shared with us some of their memorable milestone passages to favourite cruising grounds. I hope that all of you will feel encouraged to follow in their wake.

My own answer to Theo's question is eight of the thirteen, with the remainder now high on my bucket list for seasons to come. I am really looking forward to translating editorial familiarity into passage reality.

See you on the water!

Jane Russell
Editor

To the Isles of Scilly

Sam Llewellyn

Carrick Roads were cool and grey, with a ruffle of breeze. But the glass was high, the forecast said there was a high pressure motionless over the top of us, and the GRIB said breezes from the east and southeast, three and four. The plan was to visit some family on Scilly, and surprise them by arriving by boat rather than by air or on the RMS *Scillonian*. We were waiting for the ebb to kick in, so I knocked up the bacon and eggs and scrubbed the dew off the decks, casting nervous glances at my watch. Falmouth to Scilly is not a passage to be taken lightly.

With most of the ebb stream still to go I hoisted the mainsail, dropped the mooring and stuck the boat's nose past Pendennis Point and into the crisp little waves chasing each other across Falmouth Bay. There were big bulk carriers anchored out here, drained of colour in the haze. The East cardinal off the Manacles tolled in my ear. The rocks tore vees out of the ebb, and the breeze moved on to the back of my neck. The tide took us past the fine granite quay at Coverack. There was no hurry - Falmouth to the Lizard is about four hours with the ebb under you. Still, the inner sense of urgency forbade an ice-cream stop, and almost instantly we were moving past Cadgwith, with its tin church and mural of the Miraculous Draught of Fishes, with a Galilean drifter full of Apostles at one end of the seine, and a modern Cadgwith boat at the other.

The conventional advice is to stay at least three miles - better still five - off the Lizard, which is justly famed for the deeply unpleasant overfalls to its south, and should be avoided in any suspicion of wind over tide. Today, though, the breeze and the ebb worked in harmony, producing perfect conditions for lobster-pot spotting; so it was safe to take an inside passage, dodging the odd rock. As we kept our SW course to avoid the shoals off Lizard Point, two French boats were hogging Ch 16 with appallingly

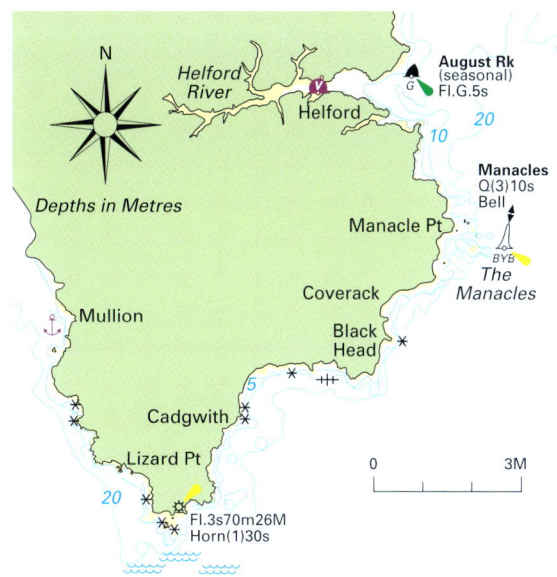

detailed discussions of the menu for their five-course Sunday lunch. The headland passed in a waft of fabric conditioner from the coaches drawn up under the lighthouse.

The open sea stretched away to the west. But it is eight hours to Scilly from here, and we are keen sleepers, and the weather forecast was still bulletproof, so instead of carrying on I hauled the tiller towards me, let go some more mainsheet, and followed the coast northwards.

The cliffs here have been hammered for thousands of years by the violent Atlantic. About five miles on, though, is Mullion, with a drying harbour inside granite quays and an offlying island. Between the quays and the island is an anchorage, popular with coasting vessels in the days of sail but not much used now, and impossible in anything but easterlies. In we turned. The anchor plunged into jade-green water, and the sound of a well-played squeezebox floated across from the deck of the elegant ketch that was our only companion. The sun went down red as blood. Rocked by a low, solid swell, we slept.

Opposite
New Grimsby harbour and Sound with Bryher in the background
Charles Tongue

Left
The anchorage at Mullion, looking south
Ian Woolcock Shutterstock

1 TO THE ISLES OF SCILLY

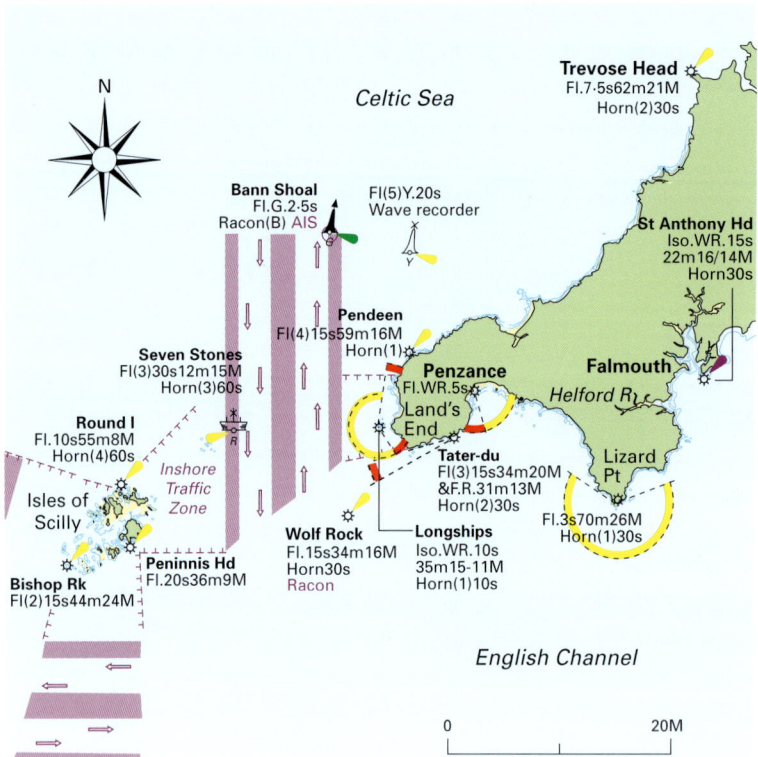

PASSAGE PLANNER
Departure from Falmouth

Standard Port Plymouth
HWS −0043   HWN −0025
LWS −0009   LWN −0009

MHWS MHWN MLWN MLWS
−0·4m −0·3m −0·4m −0·3m

Check for an outlook of settled, stable weather and plan to arrive at the Isles of Scilly in daylight. Westwards from the Lizard, Wolf Rock lighthouse (Fl.15s34m16M Horn(1)30s) is a useful passage mark. From Penzance or Newlyn leave the Runnel Stone S.Cardinal buoy to starboard and give a wide berth to the Longships rocks (Longships lighthouse (Fl(2)WR.10s35m15/11M Horn(1)10s)) 1M west of Land's End. A N-S Traffic Separation Scheme (TSS) lies between Longships and the Seven Stones reef. This notorious reef is a hazard in the NE approaches to Scilly. Land's End at around half ebb (HW Dover − 3 hours) maximises the use of the tide.

Next morning dawned pale and milky. We stowed the anchor carefully, with the pin and double lashings. The air was warm, but the swell was heaving on the rocky flanks of the island. I pointed the nose across the feeble remnants of the flood at the consolingly flat horizon a little north of west.

West of the Lizard there is no longer any pretence that this is coastal sailing. If you miss Scilly, it is next stop America. Large numbers of boats set out from Falmouth every year. Many of them change their minds early in the voyage, pull a quick 180° and head for the more crowded joys of the mainland. Ninety-nine percent of these decisions are the result of good seamanship and pure common sense.

Porth Conger, Scilly
Antony Wells

Today we would be broad-reaching, if the wind held, as the GRIB and the high, steady glass insisted it would. The lee side dug in, and the wake was a pleasant rustle as we hurdled the low swell. The log said 6·5, and we would be getting a helping hand from the slackish streams in Mount's Bay.

The Wolf Rock passed to port before lunch. The modern light is a tower of dovetailed granite. In the early 19th century it bore a bronze wolf's head, which howled dismally as the breeze played in its jaws. Like the Runnel Stone beacon and the first Bishop Rock, this was washed away early in its career - and was misplaced anyway, as the 'wolf' in its name is not lupine, but derives from the Saxon 'yulf', meaning 'gulf'.

Land's End faded into the haze to the northeast. A nervous hollow developed in my stomach. There was no sign of any islands, and we had no US visas. But the RMS *Scillonian* cruised past, and from time to time aircraft buzzed to and fro like wasps heading for invisible jamjars, so we were forced to assume that Scilly must be out here somewhere. Meanwhile, plenty of big ships were turning round the bottom left-hand corner of England, not all of them keeping watch in the Land's End TSS. We did our best to sail at right angles to the lanes while the tide shoved us first south, then, later, north.

After some six hours someone shouted, 'Land Ho!' Archaic, you may say, but you could see her point. Above the blurry horizon there now stood a row of little brown crests which did not move. We put a bit more north in the course, and gradually the hummocks joined and became a

10 Rites of Passage

mass of islands, with the red-and-white striped daymark standing proud on the easternmost moor of St Martin's.

The normal method of arriving at Scilly is to sail clockwise round St Mary's and pick up a mooring in the harbour. Because I am an enthusiast of Tresco, however, and am reluctant to sail a boat that draws 1·5m round the islands at lowish water, we had decided to leave the islands to port and sail northabout, leaving St Martin's, St Helen's, Round Island and Tresco to port, to pick up one of the excellent mooring buoys off New Grimsby.

The tide had turned, and there were some nasty bumps where the breeze blew over it round the north of Tresco. But at last we turned to port round the sucking molar of the Kettle, and dropped the sails as we slid between Tresco and Bryher. Here, in the reflection of Cromwell's Castle, we picked up a yellow buoy from water like blue satin and breathed in the waft of honeysuckle from the land.

The white tower of Round Island lighthouse is a useful daymark for a northabout arrival
Graham Adam

The blue satin waters between Tresco and Bryher, in the reflection of Cromwell's Castle
Graham Adam

1 TO THE ISLES OF SCILLY

Hazards

The islands are well charted but many of the hazards are not marked and may only be visible at LW. The golden rule when navigating within the islands is to sail on a flood tide, preferably with the sun behind you.

The islands are exposed and low lying. In unsettled weather, conditions can change very quickly. None of the anchorages are protected from all directions, so you need to be prepared to move at short notice.

Arrival at Isles of Scilly

Standard Port Plymouth

St Mary's

HWS	−0105	HWN	−0052
LWS	−0048	LWN	−0045
MHWS	MHWN	MLWN	MLWS
+0·2m	−0·1m	−0·2m	−0·1m

Southabout St Mary's, via St Mary's Sound and St Mary's Road, is the most straightforward entry from the east. The channel is buoyed and can be used, with care, in poor visibility. Note that a westerly swell can break heavily on the ledges at the northwest end of the passage and a strong E-SE wind against tide in the Sound can be rough and unpleasant. Crow Sound to the north of St Mary's is an alternative approach but is tidally restricted. However, in good visibility and with enough water it is more sheltered from the prevailing W and SW winds.

Useful fixed navigational marks are the unlit daymarks of the old white lighthouse building on St Agnes (49m) and the red and white horizontally banded daymark (56m) at the northeast end of St Martin's. One or both of these can, in reasonable visibility, be seen on most of the approaches. Another useful mark is the white tower of Round Island lighthouse (Fl.10s55m18M), particularly when making a northern landfall to one of the two best anchorages in the islands – at New Grimsby or in St Helen's Pool between Old Grimsby and St Martin's.

Tresco Abbey Gardens
Graham Adam

WHY VISIT SCILLY?

I am prejudiced in favour of the Isles of Scilly, because I was born on the island of Tresco. But just about everyone who has ever visited the place, born there or not, is prejudiced in favour of Scilly.

The land and seascape do it on their own: sea of deep-ocean clarity over glittering white sand made largely from ground-up rock crystal, and air of such purity that the colours - already Caribbean in their intensity - look twice as real as life. And given that this air is usually moving at high speed from the west, it means that the number of people on the islands is small, as is the number of yachts that arrive there.

The special attributes of Tresco, apart from my sentimental attachment to the place, are that it has the best anchorages in the archipelago, in the form of New Grimsby and St Helen's Pool between Old Grimsby and St Martin's. The bathing beaches are excellent, if you can stand water at 16°C. The moors to the north of the island are wild and beautiful, and the dunes to its south warm and filled with wild agapanthus. Also, there is an excellent pub, and, twenty minutes' walk from New Grimsby Quay, one of

12 Rites of Passage

Blockhouse Point
Tresco
Graham Adam

the greatest gardens in the world, stretching over sixteen acres and peculiarly maritime in theme.

The garden was founded by my ancestor Augustus Smith, who took over the islands from the Duchy of Cornwall in 1834, a time when they were infested with smugglers and other lowlifes. This mob gave the place a romantic air, but their depredations meant that the populace lived largely on sea beef, otherwise limpets, a kind of sushi low in nutrition and high in yuk factor. Smith consolidated the farms, improved the housing and got rid of the undesirables. He also noticed that large numbers of ships came by, many of them carrying plants destined for Kew, at that time the horticultural engine of Empire.

He became a familiar sight in a gig rowed by six strong Scillonians, ransacking the holds of passing ships for botanical treasure. What he found he brought back and planted in his garden, which since it is a couple of hundred yards from the Gulf Stream is not subject to frost. It has justly been called Kew with the Lid Off.

Scilly's Western Rocks interpose fearsome hedges of granite between Britain and the Atlantic, and the wrecks they have caught with their gales and tide rips are innumerable. The statuary in the garden at Tresco, among the tree ferns, cacti, bottlebrushes and proteas, is in fact the figureheads of wrecks, and the best examples stand in Valhalla, a melancholy loggia under the eye of bronze cannons.

The Scillonian affection for wreck is not confined to the garden. An eighteenth-century Tresco parson, caught in mid-sermon by news of a wreck, hurtled from his pulpit casting surplice and cassock away from him and shouting at the backs of his running congregation 'Start fair! In God's name, start fair!'. After a particularly interesting wreck, the houses of the neighbouring island of Bryher each had its own harmonium, and the hardy fisherfolk smelled strongly of expensive French scent. More recently, the wreck of a timber ship mysteriously coincided with the building of a large wooden extension on the New Inn, Tresco's not particularly new but uniformly excellent pub.

Figureheads and planks are not the only unusual visitors to Scilly. On the big freshwater pools of Tresco the bird life can be astonishing, and the odds of running into a crowd of twitchers bristling with lenses and aerials is high. A Greenland falcon may drop in from its native Iceland, to the consternation of the local ducks. A while ago the same pools provided bed and breakfast for something called a purple gallinule, a clumsy sort of giant moorhen that must have lumbered in from the southeastern states of the USA, goodness knows how.

Over all these natural and historical wonders lies the fact that this is a beautifully-conducted and car-free island on which children can and do run wild in perfect safety. If the effort of getting there seems a bit much - for most of the year it involves a punishing flog to windward over seas that have had seasoned P&O masters reaching for the bucket - the joy of arrival and hanging out in the islands is all the more intense. For anyone who doesn't feel up to the return trip, there is a helicopter service to Penzance. But the odds are that the voyage back to the mainland in your boat will be a downwind sleigh-ride; and that you will get the tide at the Lizard bang on.

Kew with the lid off
Mike Lewin-Harris

1 TO THE ISLES OF SCILLY

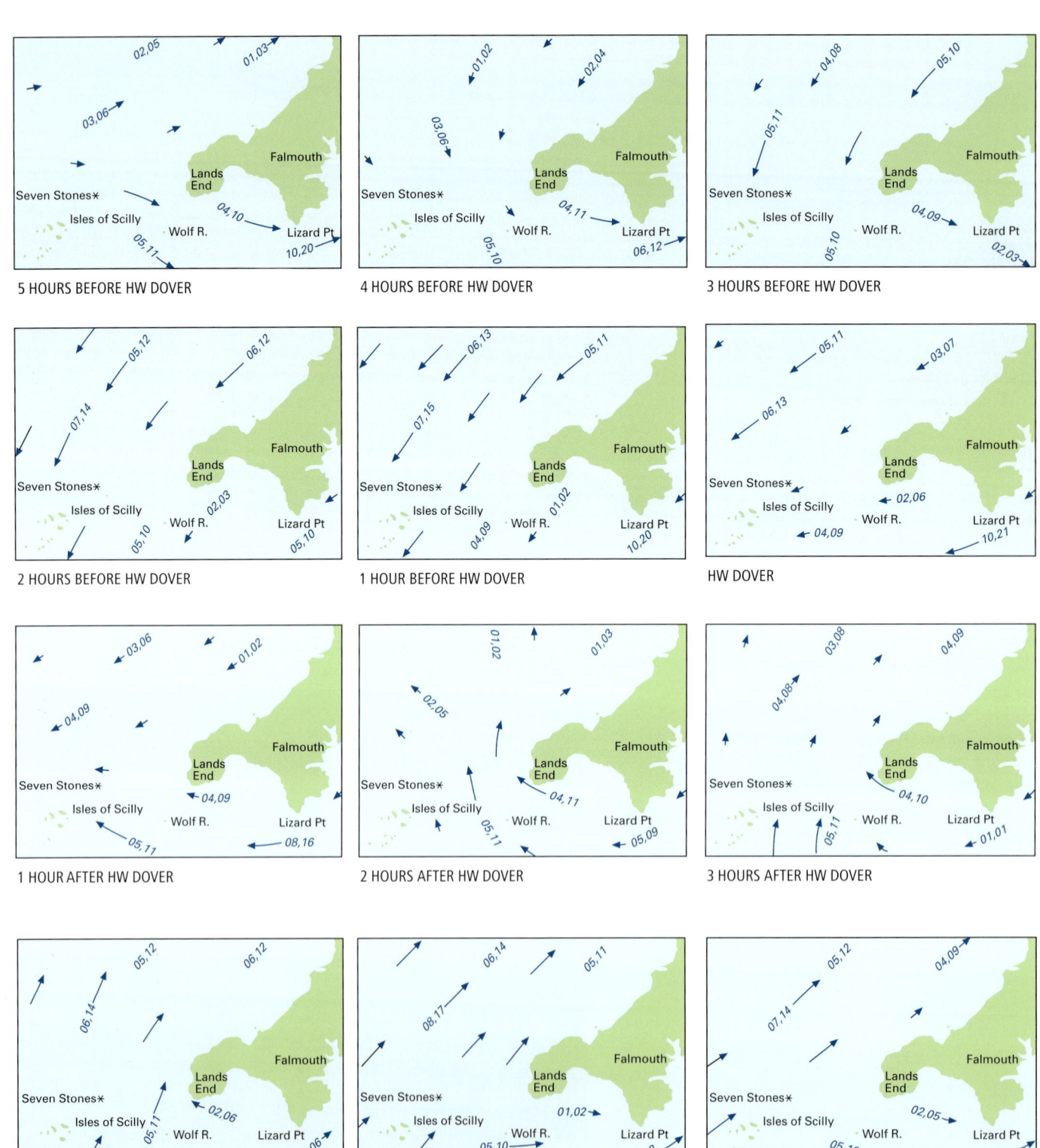

TIDAL STREAMS

The figures shown against the arrows are the mean rates at neaps and springs in tenths of a knot. Thus 07,15 - mean neaps rate 0·7 knots, mean springs rate 1·5 knots

IMRAY TIDES PLANNER

Imray Tides Planner app is a useful planning tool. Download from the App Store or Google Play.

FALMOUTH TO NEW GRIMSBY VIA MULLION

Old Grimsby Sound with St Helen's Pool beyond
Peter Russell

About the author

SAM LLEWELLYN is a Scillonian by birth, was brought up by the sea in North Norfolk, and keeps his boat near the family bothy in Tighnabruaich. He has written many nautical thrillers, large numbers of columns and stories for newspapers and magazines at home and abroad, and is the editor and founder of the Marine Quarterly (www.marinequarterly.com) . He has recently hauled back from the jaws of dereliction a heavy Deep Seadog ketch, in which he cruises the west coast of Scotland and anywhere else that rises from the horizon.

For more about Sam's work, visit www.samllewellyn.com

Imray books and charts

Isles of Scilly
Graham Adam / Royal Cruising Club Pilotage Foundation (Imray)
A must for anyone planning an extended visit to this beautiful archipelago on the edge of the Atlantic

The West Country
Carlos Rojas and Susan Kemp-Wheeler (Imray)
Covering Lyme Bay to Land's End and the Isles of Scilly it provides essential sailing directions and detailed listings of facilities together with a wealth of information for those wishing to learn about the West Country and enjoy trips ashore.

Chart packs (paper and digital)
2400 West Country

Planning charts
C18 Western approaches to English Channel   1:1,000,000
C10 Western English Channel passage chart   1:400,000

Passage charts
C7 Falmouth to Isles of Scilly and Trevose Head   1:120,000

Harbour chart
Y58 River Fal   1:20,000
Y47 Falmouth Harbour   1:20,000
Y49 Isles of Scilly   1:40,000
Y50 St Mary's, Tresco and Surrounding Islands   1:20,000

Imray Digital
ID20 English Channel
ID30 West Britain and Ireland

Rites of Passage **15**

Across Lyme Bay

Megan Clay

LULWORTH TO SALCOMBE

It seems to be one of the unwritten rules of sailing that catching a tide always involves a deplorably early start. A bleary-eyed swinging of legs out of the bunk and the shock of warm toes on the chill cabin sole, which sends you stumbling to silence the offending alarm clock. Or perhaps it is just that my passage making is always shoehorned into borrowed hours, every fair weather window and tide taken advantage of to maximise time in the next cruising ground.

So it was that we had left our mooring in Chichester Harbour at dawn, played snakes and ladders against the tide off Hurst Castle, and then revelled in a sunny afternoon fetching and beating westward past Durlston and St Alban's Head. Finally, reluctantly, we stowed the sails and fired up the engine to nose into Lulworth Cove after the end of the breeze and with the last of the light.

The next morning the alarm once again hauls us from sleep and we drowsily make ready for sea. The engine seems embarrassingly loud in the crisp morning air as it pushes the bows through their own inky-blue reflections in search of the anchor.

Outside, the breeze slowly fills in from the southwest and we start to sail. Ahead of us lurks Portland Race where, for 10 of every 12 hours, strong south-bound streams down the Isle of Portland collide with the east- or west-going Channel tide and kick up over Portland Ledge. In strong winds it is not uncommon for the sea state to become very dangerous. Today the tides are neapy and the breeze is light. We want to carry a tide across Lyme Bay so we have timed our transit past Portland Bill at five hours after High Water Plymouth. We are hoping Portland Race will be easy-going but we've double-checked the hatches are closed.

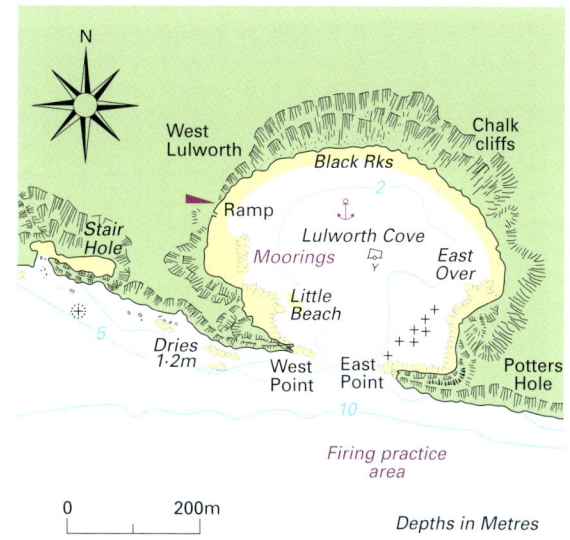

Deciding to take the inner passage, we sneak close inshore to ride the tide down the eastern side of Portland, short-tacking the final mile until we are under the lighthouse. We dodge the lobster pots as we stand on as long as we dare, facing the warm glow of early morning sunshine on the cliffs.

We tack out again towards Portland Ledge and hit a bit of a chop, but happily nothing to justify our precautions. A final tack and we're past Portland Bill and fetching well out into Lyme Bay. The kettle goes on again for a celebratory second breakfast of coffee with *pain aux raisins*. Our

Far left
The distinctive white stripes of Portland Bill mark a key division of the South Coast
Megan Clay

Below
Lulworth Cove
Shaun Jacobs / Dreamstime

Rites of Passage **17**

2 ACROSS LYME BAY

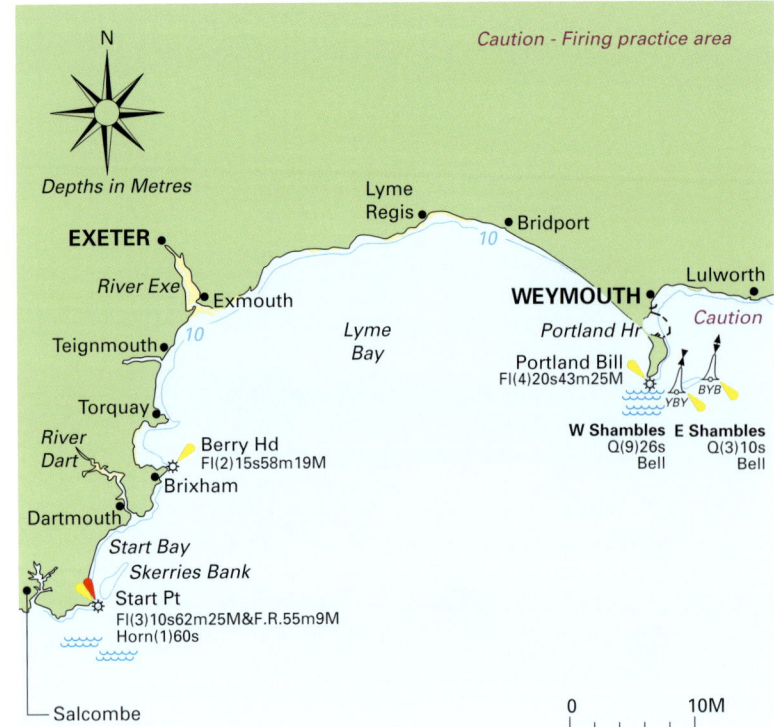

PASSAGE PLANNER
Departure from Lulworth

Standard Port Portland
HWS +0015   HWN +0005
LWS −0005   LWN 0000
MHWS MHWN MLWN MLWS
+0·1m   +0·1m +0·2m +0·1m

This almost circular cove, with its narrow entrance, is an ideal overnight spot before tackling Portland Race, but if there is any chance of the wind going into the S, it would be wise to move before any swell, potentially dangerous, rolls in. In these conditions Portland or Weymouth are a better option.

Severe sea states can occur in Portland Race which usually extends 2M south of Portland Bill (Fl(4)20s43m25M) but much further in bad weather. Aim for slackish water off the Bill at HW Plymouth +5 to HW −5, which becomes a favourable tide for the west-bound passage. In daylight and settled conditions, the inshore passage provides a shorter route around the Bill in relatively flat water.

To take this route, position yourself close inshore at least 2M north of the Bill to ride the south-going stream. Then keep 1 to 3 cables off the Bill to stay clear of Portland Ledge and avoid being set into the Race. At night, with wind against tide, or in fresh onshore breezes, avoid the Race by passing at least 3M south of the Bill.

Hazards

There is a firing practice area, used by both the army and navy, from St Alban's Head to approx 5M S of Lulworth Cove.

Lulworth Gunnery Range (army) info from
☎ 01929 404819 (recording) or
☎ 01929 404700

Naval Firing-range safety boats, VHF 08 and 16, are stationed at the edges of the danger area. Firing times are broadcast by the coastguard and Radio Solent.
24hr pre-recorded message on
☎ 01929 404819

mood is clearly infectious – we had hoped we might see dolphins, and we are in luck. A pod joins us, playing under our bow.

It is 55 miles to Salcombe from Portland Bill, so while the days are long and the tides favourable, it should be possible for us to make the passage during daylight hours. Our plan is to head straight across, pushing the last of the east-going tide off Start Point or, if our speed drops a little, enjoying slack water over the last few miles across Lannacombe Bay. If the wind dies, we'll head to Brixham for some sleep.

The sail across Lyme Bay will put us out of sight of land for several hours and will feel truly offshore for almost as long as a Channel crossing. For this reason, and the two potential ferocious headlands at either end, it really is a rite of passage.

We make a respectable 5 knots through the water, close-hauled, as Portland Bill shrinks into the distance. The breeze backs and we think we

Dolphins join in across Lyme Bay
Megan Clay

might lay Start Point, so we relax into straight-line sailing against the gentle pull of the tiller. There isn't much out here to avoid, just the outline of the odd fishing boat in the distance. Beyond our horizon to the north, Lyme Regis passes with lunch. Exmouth also passes far to leeward.

Last time we were heading this way we stopped in for a night, but the wind and tides don't always line up so nicely and this time we are pushing on. Start Point grows steadily bigger through the afternoon until we can make out Slapton Sands stretching away to the north. Our thoughts turn to April 1944 when Exercise Tiger,

18 Rites of Passage

LULWORTH TO SALCOMBE

Salcombe buzzes with activity
Peter Russell

one of several rehearsals here for D-Day, ended in catastrophe and the deaths of more than 700 Americans. Troops practising beach landings came under friendly fire and then, out in the bay, one of the rehearsing convoys came under attack from German E-boats. This afternoon, though, the Devon coastline is tranquil, and by tea time Start Point is a mile or so off. We steal tentatively inshore in search of the first of the southwest going tide, keeping an eye on the swell breaking gently on the rocks below the lighthouse. Sitting warm in the afternoon sun, I remember a rather different day last year when I ran the spectacular coastal path from Hallsands out to the point. An autumn gale had whipped up the race and there were white horses stretching far offshore, gulls wheeling in the spray of the breaking waves.

As we leave Start Point behind us we begin to close the coastguard huts of Prawle Point with Salcombe harbour beyond. We aim to keep far enough south to avoid Rickham Rock, a few cables short of the bar. Once again the breeze is dying by the time we reach the entrance. We are now only a couple of hours before low tide, but there is plenty of water on the bar. We bear away off Starehole Bay and push slowly north on the

Smalls Cove, Salcombe
Peter Russell

Rites of Passage **19**

2 ACROSS LYME BAY

Arrival at Salcombe

Standard Port Plymouth

HWS	−0010	HWN	+0000
LWS	+0005	LWN	−0005
MHWS	MHWN	MLWN	MLWS
−0·2m	−0·3m	−0·1m	−0·1m

Start Point (Fl(3)10s62m25MHorn60s), with its distinctive cock's comb spine and white lighthouse, also has a race which may extend 1.5M east and 1M to the south. In bad weather you should keep at least 2M off. The entrance to Salcombe is just to the east of Bolt Head, with its spiky silhouette and the offlying Mewstone and Little Mewstone to the SE.

In settled weather, entry to Salcombe is straightforward. However, dangerous breakers can occur on the bar (least depth 1m) in strong onshore winds or swell, particularly when the tide is on the ebb, making entry impossible. If you are unsure, call the Harbourmaster on VHF 14 for guidance. The red and white leading marks on Sandhill Point (Dir.Fl.WRG.2s27m8M) and the Poundstone will take you in on 000° over the bar and past Bass Rock (Fl.R.5s). Further channel buoys guide you past Wolf Rock (Fl.G.5s) and between Blackstone Rock to starboard and Poundstone to port, where you turn onto the 042·5° inner lead.

It is possible to anchor at Sunny Cove, off Smalls Cove and further up the river. Visitors' moorings off the town can be boisterous in a southerly when better shelter can be found on moorings further up in The Bag.

leading line against the ebb, then gybe and ghost up towards Mill Bay, where it looks like it's Merlin Week, with a host of dinghies on the beach and smoke rising from several barbecues. Sunny Cove is honouring its name and the forecast is good, so beyond the Blackstone we round up to starboard to drop anchor in the clear water.

All packed up, we cradle a glass of ale and enjoy the evening sun as it dips towards the trees on Moult Point. Tomorrow we might explore up river towards Kingsbridge, take the dinghy up one of the creeks, or just head into town in search of a cream tea. I certainly have no intention of being up at dawn ...

Plenty of enticements along Salcombe's narrow lanes
Peter Russell

WHY VISIT ?

Once across Lyme Bay you are truly in the West Country - a treat for sailors and landlubbers alike. The far southwest of England is not only replete with characterful seaside towns and fishing ports, you can also stock up on local beverages from orchards and nascent vineyards, eat your fill of locally caught seafood, or locally produced ice cream, and argue good-naturedly with your crew about which should be applied first to your freshly baked scones – the jam or the clotted cream.

If you want to stretch your legs, the South West Coast Path is your constant companion, meandering along clifftops and sand dunes from Poole Harbour in Dorset all the way round to Minehead on the north Devon coast. Or you can swap cruiser for paddleboard, kayak or dinghy to explore rias, rivers and creeks.

With roots in fishing, boatbuilding and seafaring, Salcombe has long made its living from the sea. Its estuary, in fact a flooded valley, or ria, saw nearly 300 sailing vessels built during the nineteenth century, almost all for local owners.

20 Rites of Passage

North Sands beach is well protected from the prevailing westerlies
Megan Clay

But by the turn of the century, boatbuilding here was already in decline, with iron and steel boats built in northern England superseding many of their wooden counterparts for international trade.

Visitors have always been attracted by Salcombe's climate and beauty, and well-heeled holidaymakers gradually replaced the boatyards. It is easy to see why; Salcombe is the perfect location for a family holiday. With sandy beaches facing east and west, there's always somewhere with good shelter to swim in the sea or build a sandcastle; the water buzzes with the activity of boats ferrying people between Salcombe and Portlemouth, dinghies under sail and tenders full of visiting cruisers; and the town comes out *en fête* throughout the summer for its numerous regattas.

On a rainy day, you can take a ferry upriver to the market town of Kingsbridge, with its independent shops, restaurants and pubs. Or stay to discover some of Salcombe's less well-known attractions, like the heated outdoor swimming pool - built in the 1970s, it is open all year round.

If sampling local fare is your priority, the town boasts an excellent bakery, fishmongers, and a clutch of delis, not to mention restaurants, cafes and pubs. The Yacht Club also welcomes visiting sailors for food and drink and enjoys a delightful view, but my own highlight remains the ice cream shops selling deliciously decadent flavours from local dairies.

For those looking to maximise their time afloat, Salcombe is well placed for relaxed hops along the coast. Daysail back east around the Start to explore the river Dart as it takes you through Dartmouth and on past Dittisham, or go further for Brixham's fresh fish, or the sandy beaches and villages of the Exe. Hopping further west, the rugged beauty of the Cornish coast isn't far away, with the Yealm or the Erme interesting stop-offs en route.

Salcombe is a perfect playground for all the family
Megan Clay

2 ACROSS LYME BAY

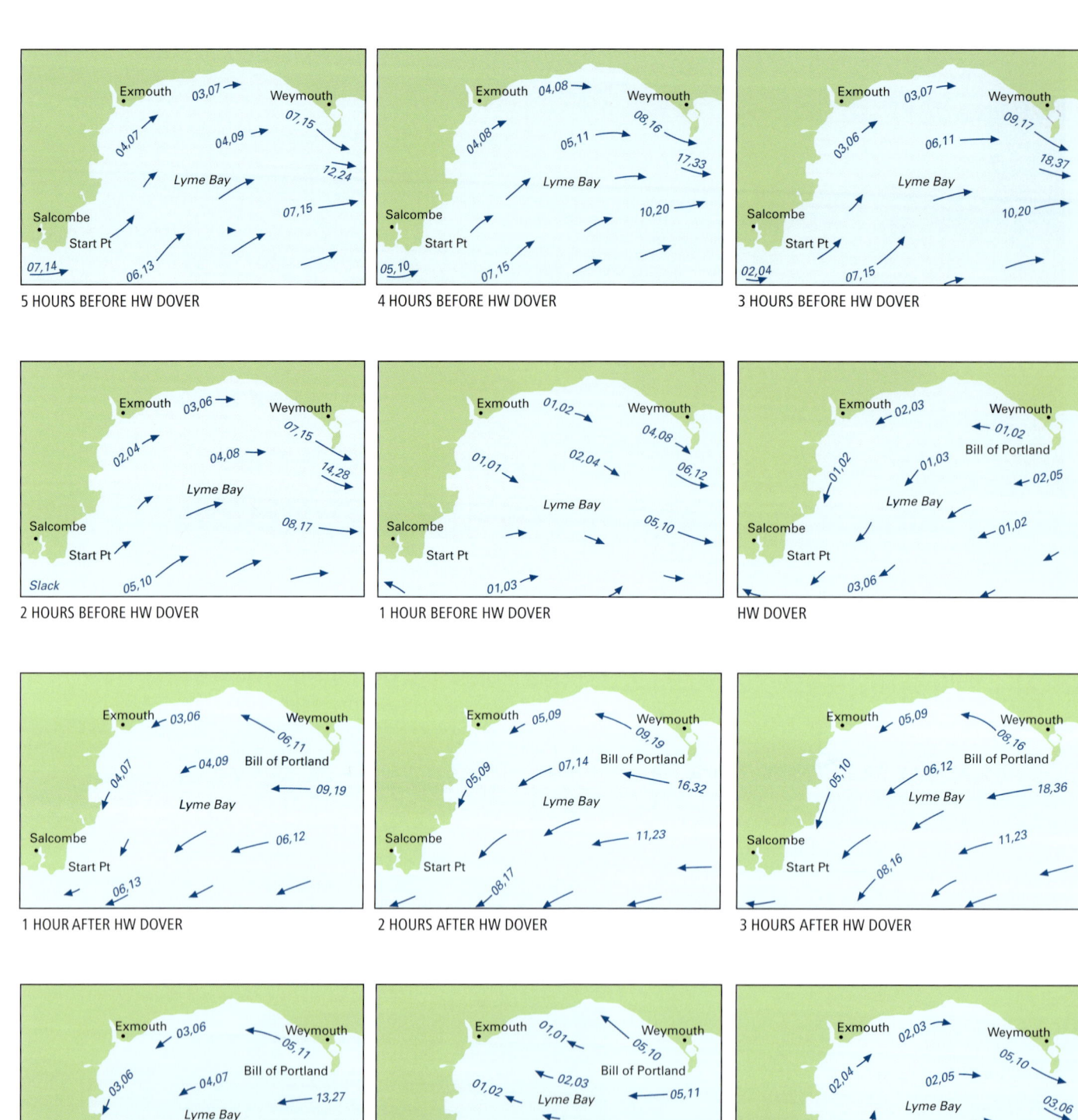

TIDAL STREAMS

The figures shown against the arrows are the mean rates at neaps and springs in tenths of a knot. Thus 07,15 - mean neaps rate 0·7 knots, mean springs rate 1·5 knots

IMRAY TIDES PLANNER

Imray Tides Planner app is a useful planning tool. Download from the App Store or Google Play.

LULWORTH TO SALCOMBE

A busy dinghy dock, typical of many West Country harbours
Peter Russell

About the author

MEGAN CLAY learnt to sail dinghies on the Exe estuary and has been sailing keelboats since 2002. As well as sailing in the west country, Megan has cruised the Baltic from the Åland Islands to Arctic Norway and, in 2015, left her job to go sailing with her husband, Ed. They took their 1973 Contessa 38 south as far as The Gambia and Cape Verde, before crossing the Atlantic to cruise the Caribbean, Bahamas, US east coast, Atlantic Canada and Greenland. Her more recent cruises have included northern Brittany and the west coast of Scotland.

Imray books and charts

The Shell Channel Pilot
Tom Cunliffe (Imray)

'Shell' is more than a harbour guide. It also provides a reassuring hand on the shoulder for Channel navigation, with useful passage notes gleaned from the compiler's personal experience of more than 40 years running the tides and finding the eddies.

The West Country
Carlos Rojas and Susan Kemp-Wheeler (Imray)

Covering Lyme Bay to Land's End and the Isles of Scilly it provides essential sailing directions and detailed listings of facilities together with a wealth of information for those wishing to learn about the West Country and enjoy trips ashore.

Chart packs (paper and digital)
2300 Dorset and Devon Coasts
2400 West Country Chart Atlas

Planning charts
C10 Western English Channel passage chart   1:400,000

Passage charts
C4	Needles Channel to Bill of Portland	1:100,000
C5	Bill of Portland to Salcombe Harbour	1:75,000
Y41	Teignmouth and Tor Bay	1:55,000
Y42	Exmouth to Salcombe	1:100,000

Harbour charts
Y40	River Exe	1:21,500
Y43	River Dart	1:15,000
Y44	Salcombe	1:15,000

Imray Digital
ID20 English Channel

Across the Thames Estuary

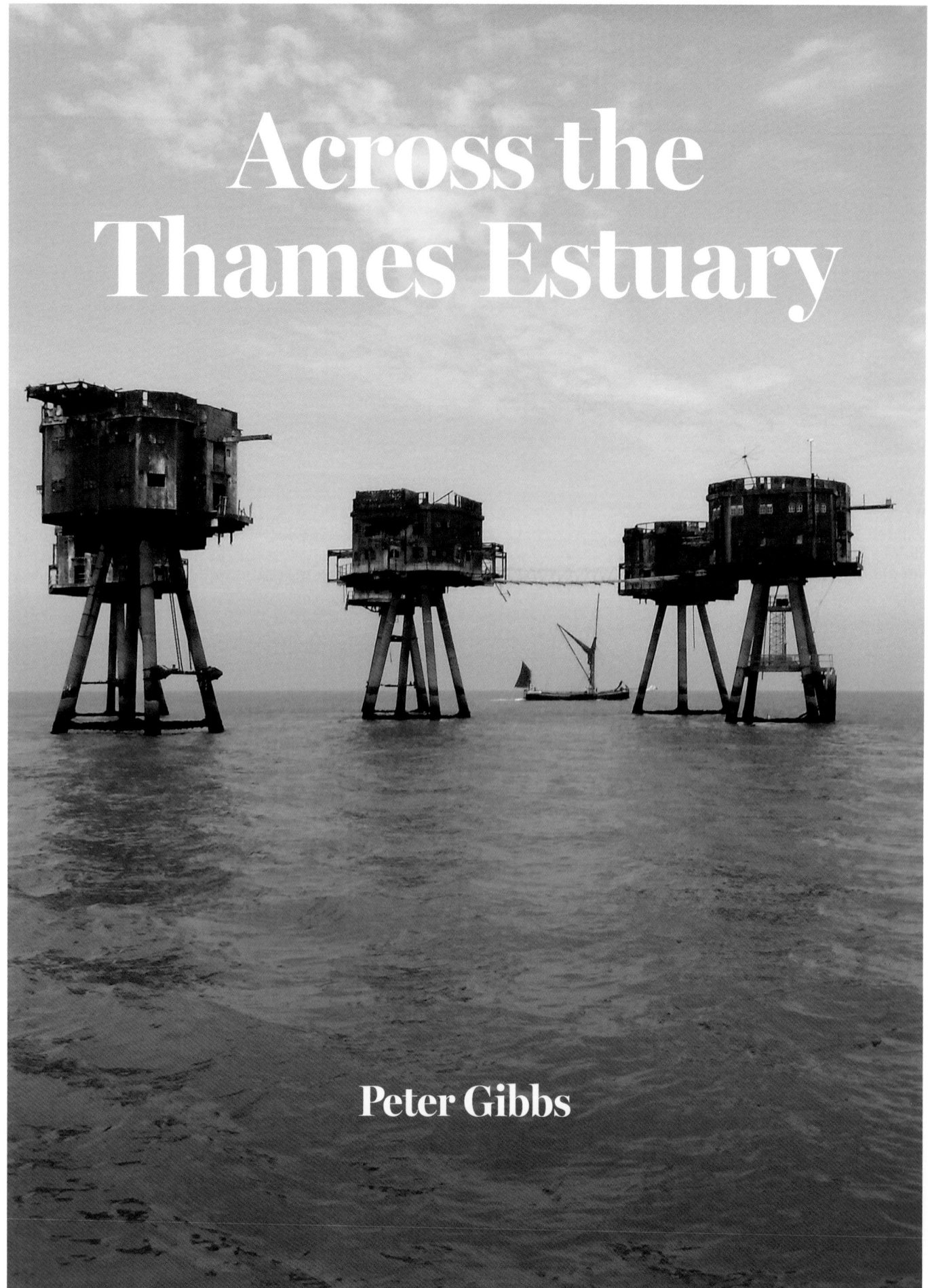

Peter Gibbs

Did I really need an excuse to make another dash across the Thames Estuary from Harwich to Ramsgate? Yes, I've done it several times over the years, but for me it's one of those must-do passages: never the same and loaded with character.

With its vigorous tides, short seas, narrow gats, and constrained passage-making, a successful Thames crossing is a satisfaction not to be found elsewhere. It's a privilege – and right on our doorstep.

It's early May and there is a hint of crispness in the spring air. The boat is in prime shape, clean of hull and well stowed. *Joelle*, my Bavaria 38 Ocean drawing 1·9 metres, is a willing Pegasus, and over several seasons has taken me to the Baltic and southwest France, quite a lot of it sailing solo, for which it's well set up. But on this occasion I set sail with Peter, my trusty club crew, complete with his rather moth-eaten woolly hat.

Joelle is berthed at Titchmarsh Marina in the Walton Backwaters, just south of Harwich. Departing at half ebb, we round the chicane at Stone Point and head out for the Pye End buoy. We have one metre under the keel for parts of the channel but in a gentle sea that doesn't disturb us unduly. At the No 2 red can, up goes the jib and full main as we turn to starboard and settle down to the northeasterly breeze which is puffing up over Force 4 on the port bow.

This is a trip we now like to finesse. Sailing out south of the Cork Sand, we spot a patch of ochre shading in the water slipping away to port, confirming the shallows on the bar in the falling tide.

Our course takes us out towards the Wallet and Peter remarks that there's hardly space under the keel for a scraper blade. Yes, but the seabed here is pretty flat, so the shallows are no threat in these conditions. The low sandy cliffs of The Naze frame the horizon to the south, and the enormous container cranes at Felixstowe sit on our transom and remain there for miles.

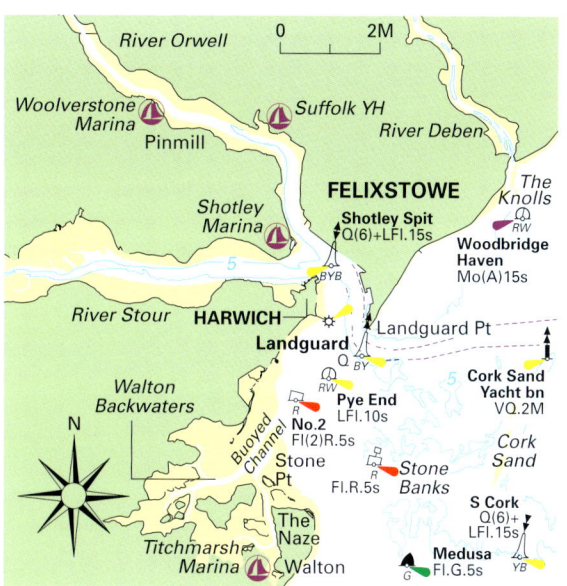

There are three major banks fanning out into the North Sea from the mouth of the Thames: Gunfleet, Sunk, and Long Sand. These moraine dumps hailing from the last Ice Age make a direct passage to the North Foreland impossible and mean that we will alternate from nothing under the keel to a full 20-metre depth in between.

The South Cork cardinal slides by to port and it has to be time for a cuppa. 'We're out of tea,' comes the plaintive call from below. No way! I direct Peter to my recently replenished stores locker.

The northeasterly breeze has come in just as the BBC forecasted and we're making over 5 knots with all sails nicely shaped. But Peter

Opposite
Heading out from Titchmarsh past the popular anchorage at Stone Point
Jane Russell

Far left
A Thames barge heads past the eerie Maunsell Forts on Red Sands
Jane Russell

3 ACROSS THE THAMES ESTUARY

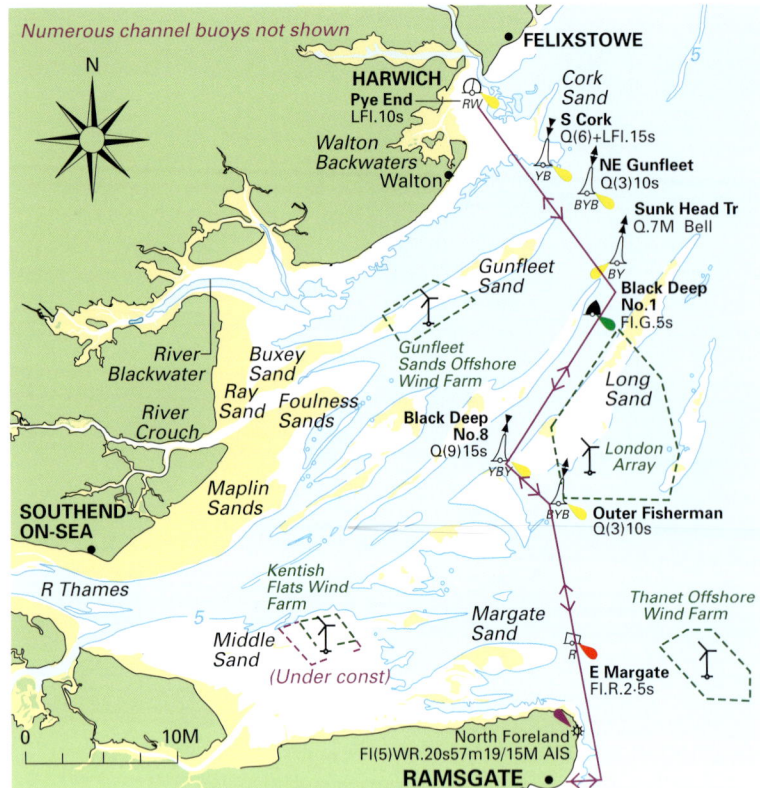

PASSAGE PLANNER

Departure from the Walton Backwaters

Standard Port Walton

HWS	+0005	HWN	+0003
LWS	–0020	LWN	–0005

MHWS	MHWN	MLWN	MLWS
+0·2m	0·0m	–0·1m	-0.1m

Leaving any of the Harwich marinas or anchorages, yachts should use the recommended yacht channels and keep watch for commercial shipping.

The SW-NE orientation of the Thames means that strong SW or NE winds can affect tide heights, times and flow. Wind against tide produces a characteristic short, steep chop which becomes unpleasant above F4. The offshore sandbanks are endlessly shifting and buoys are frequently moved, so even up-to-date charts should be used with caution. However, waves breaking on the banks can be seen from some distance, and you can use the tides to your advantage. The flood runs SW into the Thames and the ebb runs NE, so leaving Harwich at half ebb helps you to stay north of the main sands as you make your easting. You then have the full benefit of the flood as you turn south. The feasibility of the outer route via Long Sand Head and down the outside of Kentish Knock will depend on the winds, but it provides fewer waymarks and takes you very close to the Sunk TSS.

Taking the inner route, from Pye End (LFl 10s) to South Cork (Q(6)+L. Fl.15s), the Naze Tower day mark watches over you to the west.

Out past NE Gunfleet (Q (3) 10s) you can start to feel isolated, but the Gunfleet Sand windfarm to the southwest should orientate you.

From Sunk Head Tower (Q.7M Whis) and down the buoyed channel of Black Deep, the London Array wind farm will guide you to Fisherman's Gat. A bearing of 173° takes you towards East Margate (Fl.R.2.5s) where the chalk cliffs beneath the white tower of the North Foreland lighthouse (Fl(5)WR.20s57m19/15M) will emerge. Keep parallel to the cliffs as you head south and aim to meet the Ramsgate channel between starboard hand No3 buoy (Fl(G)2.5s) and southerly cardinal No5 (Q(6)+ LFl.15s).

Leaving Ramsgate for Harwich, pick up the start of the north-going flow about 1 hr before HW Dover and carry the ebb before picking up the flood into the Orwell or Walton Backwaters.

enjoys working the sheets, so I look the other way while he ensures that we derive every watt of power from the breeze. Even slightly quavering roaches are taboo, it seems.

We carry the ebb, lee-bowing, which keeps us clear of Gunfleet Sand with its forest of windmills, and The Sunk, which has so far been spared the pile driver. The outer route, east of the Long Sand, would entail a further five miles of eastings, close on the breeze for no other gain, so it's not for us today.

I have reckoned this trip will take about seven hours for the 45 miles to Ramsgate. You could just follow the chartplotter, but I prefer to exercise old skills by working the course, aided by the numerous buoys and the new man-made scenery of wind farms along the route. I know from experience that the estuary is pretty well buoyed – well enough, indeed, to sail even in quite poor visibility.

Setting off at half ebb allows us enough time to reach our turning point at the Sunk, close on low water. We aim for half way between the Black Deep No 1 (G) buoy and the Sunk Head northerly cardinal mark, easing ourselves over

The low sandy cliffs under the Naze tower frame the horizon
Jane Russell

26 Rites of Passage

North Foreland emerges through the light haze
Peter Gibbs

the gently sloping sands, working the contours on the depth gauge. These sands do shift, but four metres minimum under us is pretty comfortable.

The flood is just getting underway as we head into the fantastically named Black Deep. The gauge begins to rise as *Joelle* cracks off southwest, ready to rock and roll, riding the flood. The GPS soon shows 8 knots over the ground. In the sunlight, the sea is lifted from its usual Thames grey-ochre to a hint of blue, reflecting the clearing sky. We are alone in the middle of the estuary, one of the most famous waterways in the world. We're slipping along its convoluted swatches, recounting segments of the long history passing beneath our keel, imagining all the gear lost into these waters over the centuries. Oh, the stories that haul could tell!

As we plunge down the Black Deep, the massive London Array wind farm straddles the Long Sand on our port side, the blades making Swiss-knife patterns as we pass the rows of pylons.

An hour and a half later we haul up to the southern edge of the array, where it's time to make the final leap across the Long Sand into free water. We begin to glide over towards the westerly cardinal marking the Fisherman's Gat, the traditional safe route across. At the edge of the Black Deep the depth starts to worry us both.

Long Sand has extended eastwards more than expected, so we correct to the west, taking a gybe and heading clear until close on the buoy.

The Fisherman's Gat is a broad waterway, well buoyed, and gives us four metres under the keel on the rising tide. Three miles across, the easterly cardinal appears, and we ease sheets and slope off south to the North Foreland, the cliffs of Kent not yet in view through the light haze.

Our penultimate marker is the East Margate (R) can, taken on our starboard and beginning to show signs of the turn of the flood stream westwards into the Thames. Two tankers hang to their chains as the Outer Thames anchorage slides by. The North Foreland light sits atop the chalk cliffs, but the approach is shallow, so we hold off 3 cables or so. The last five miles run into Ramsgate brings us home in just a tad over one tide. Ramsgate Port grants us entry and we drop sails inside the outer harbour.

Ramsgate presents a special maritime charm, with its Victorian facade of red-bricked cliffs sporting rows of shops and eateries underneath the archways, amongst them is the Royal Temple Yacht Club. With its mass of exotic trophies on display, it exudes tradition and extends its welcome to all passing sailors. Peter and I feel well rewarded by its warm embrace.

Windfarms in the Thames Estuary have become a new aid to navigation
Shutterstock / Kaisn

3 ACROSS THE THAMES ESTUARY

Arrival at Ramsgate

Standard Port Dover

HWS	+0030	HWN	+0030
LWS	+0007	LWN	+0017
MHWS	MHWN	MLWN	MLWS
−1·6m	−1·3m	−0·7m	−0·2m

Yachts should report to Ramsgate Port Control on VHF 14 before entering the harbour. Once inside the harbour, leave Harbour (Q.G) buoy to starboard and turn north through the entrance into Royal Harbour. For pontoon berths in the western marina, turn to port around the end of the harbour wall, keeping a sharp lookout for any vessels leaving the marina. Call Ramsgate Marina on VHF 80.

WHY CROSS THE THAMES?

Thames voyagers never suffer from déjà vu – they are spoilt for a range of destinations. Given wind, tide and inclination we could have passaged from Harwich to a number of attractive and interesting ports dotted around the estuary, each a living witness to its formative place in the history of England. Just about any are attainable on one long tide from Harwich or Ramsgate; channels are well marked throughout and key havens are all tide.

A passage south from Harwich would skirt the western flank of the Gunfleet Sand, nipping over the Swin Spitway into Middle Deep and you are borne swiftly past Maplin Sands towards the River Medway on one tide. In stronger wind conditions we would have broken off and made port in Essex at Brightlingsea or further inland at Maldon on the Blackwater. Both are restricted by tide but home to the remains of the Thames barge fleet, built with shallow draught for coastal cargo traffic but now enjoyed by passengers taking the sea air on sunny days. Close by, the River Crouch is a veritable citadel of class yacht racing, overseen by Burnham, backed up by well-established and welcoming sailing clubs and satisfying food. A favourite destination with good marina accommodation.

The warm embrace of Ramsgate
Christine Bird / Dreamstime

28 Rites of Passage

Perfect tranquillity on the River Stour
Jane Russell

Arriving at the Medway, the main feature is the historic Chatham Dockyard - visitable from the two nearby locking marinas. For several hundred years Chatham and the Medway were the hub of British east coast naval resources - now a museum site. The sense of naval history on the Medway is powerful, especially at the entrance as you pass the wreck of the SS *Richard Montgomery*, nursing its rotting cargo of explosives for over 70 years. The Medway is eerily quiet these days but is slowly recovering from the post war retreat of navy, industry and commerce.

Starting out north from Ramsgate or Dover presents yet other opportunities, all within a tide's reach. Rounding the North Foreland lies the charming town of Margate, an open harbour for boats that can take the ground. This town is on the rise with the whole of Thanet and boasts Turner Contemporary gallery, named after the father of British impressionism. In days of sail, many a wooden tall ship waited off here for favourable wind before heading down channel to explore and trade.

Further west, past Reculver Towers, lies historic Whitstable, accessed over the flats on a rising tide but a harbour where you must be prepared to take the ground – a polite term for a lot of mud. But oysters are still sought after here, 2000 years after the Romans began the trade, although the volumes are not quite what they were in Dickensian times.

The Isle of Sheppey presents next, separated from Kent by the Swale, a winding waterway leading to Queenborough at the western end - a quiet haven sheltered from most points of the wind and a fine leaping off point for the trip up to Harwich, but also long favoured by vessels taking the tide upriver to London Bridge.

Off the Essex coast the historic brick light tower on the Naze is a sure guide to the River Orwell entrance, with the option to turn at Pye End into the Walton Backwaters, with Titchmarsh marina close to hand. The birdlife established on the extensive mudflats is impressive. Dovercourt Bay, off Harwich, was once a racing ground for J-class yachts and Harwich itself, was a packet station connecting England to the continent for centuries – a ferry service continues the link to this day. Rivers Stour and Orwell offer unspoilt rolling wooded waterways running miles inland, and sporting numerous marinas and clubs.

North of Harwich the almost untouched waterways of the River Deben and Ore are available to those prepared to sail over protective entrance bars, awash at low water. The Ore reaches inland, past Aldeborough to Snape Maltings, home of the world-famous music festivals.

The literature born of the Thames and its many faces and ports is significant and enriches understanding of the unique heritage. For sailors, few accounts have bettered those of Maurice Griffiths relating his adventures around the estuary from nearly a century ago. Passaging the swatchways between the banks was an art form; the picture painted was of near nonchalance and leisured sailing, for when the wind got up apparently all you had to do was slip into the lee of a sandbank and drop anchor, let the bank take the weather strain until it all passed by. Heroic style.

The Thames estuary may appear a paradox of ever varying depths, numerous wind farms and natural obstacles, hosting a major world waterway, and yet as likely you will not have to share your crossing with another yacht the whole voyage. What a privilege to enjoy access to such an asset and at the end of the journey to spot the ancient chalk cliffs of Kent or the modern cranes of Felixstowe emerge from the distance to round off another deeply satisfying passage of this ancient waterway.

3 ACROSS THE THAMES ESTUARY

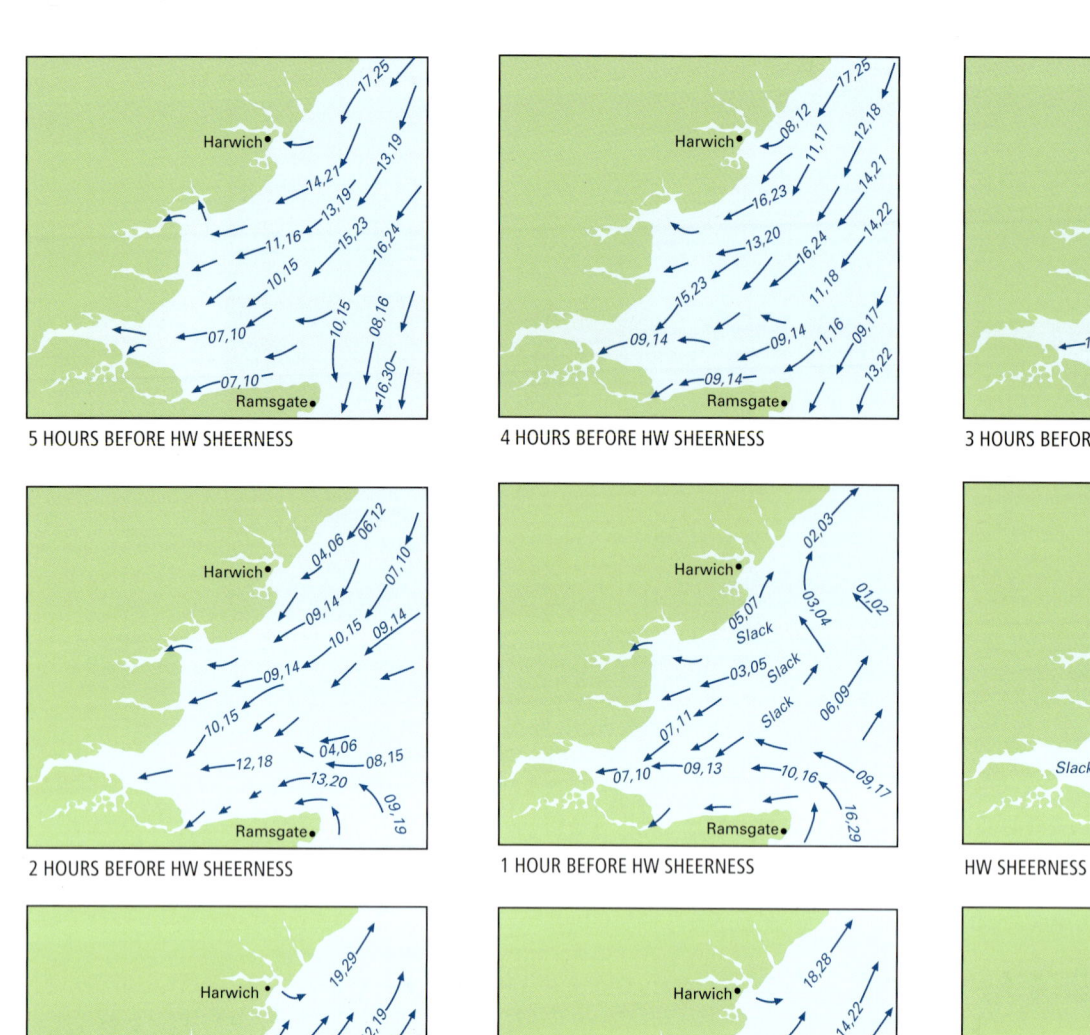

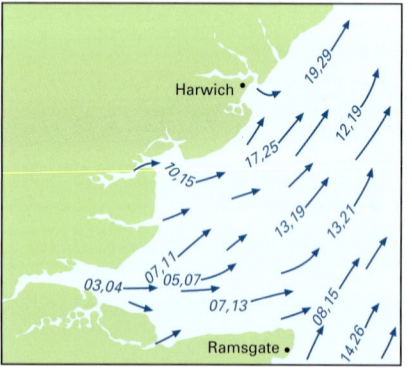
1 HOUR AFTER HW SHEERNESS

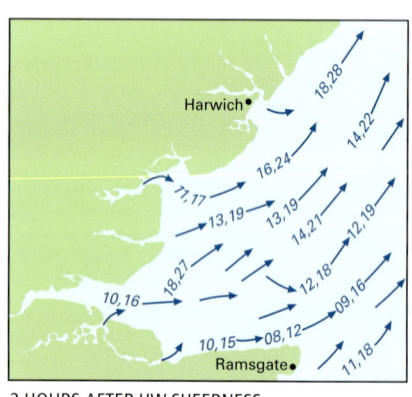
2 HOURS AFTER HW SHEERNESS

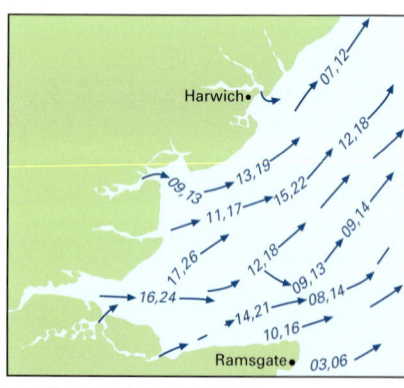
3 HOURS AFTER HW SHEERNESS

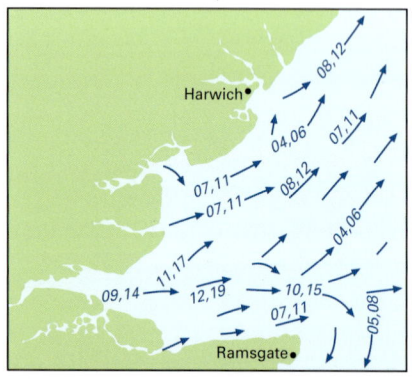
4 HOURS AFTER HW SHEERNESS

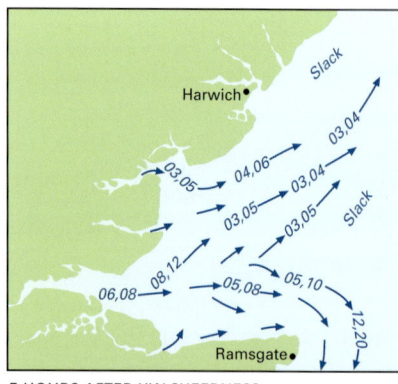
5 HOURS AFTER HW SHEERNESS

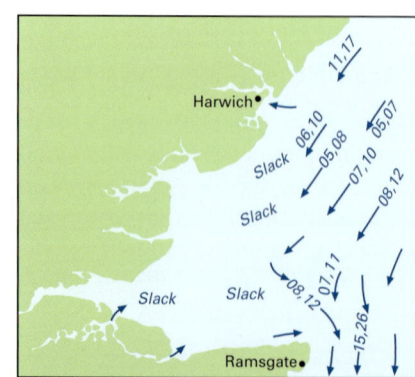
6 HOURS AFTER HW SHEERNESS

TIDAL STREAMS

The figures shown against the arrows are the mean rates at neaps and springs in tenths of a knot. Thus 07,15 - mean neaps rate 0·7 knots, mean springs rate 1·5 knots

IMRAY TIDES PLANNER

Imray Tides Planner app is a useful planning tool. Download from the App Store or Google Play.

Rites of Passage

WALTON BACKWATERS TO RAMSGATE

The Rocks anchorage on the River Deben is another popular spot
Jane Russell

About the author

PETER GIBBS learned boat handling as a youngster on family holidays at Whitstable and the thrill of boating never left him. Later, when his daughters had grown, he took the plunge at the London Boat Show and bought a day boat. He traded up to a Westerly Fulmar to stretch his range around southern England and the continent. Following his retirement, Peter took his Bavaria 38 Ocean, *Joelle*, and further extended his sailing to the Baltic and southwest France. This boat, Peter exclaims, will 'probably be my last', and is named after his forgiving wife. He says that Holland remains his favourite foreign destination for sailing, but its neighbours are extremely appealing too.

Imray books and charts

East Coast Pilot
Garth Cooper and Dick Holness (Imray)
The bible for cruising sailors for the waters between Great Yarmouth and Ramsgate. Not only does it cover the many harbours, rivers and creeks in a clear and concise manner, it also reveals some of the mysteries of sailing these shallow and shifting coastal waters, with unique 'rolling road' diagrams to guide the approach showing buoyage sequences and tracks to steer into rivers and ports.

Crossing the Thames Estuary
Roger Gaspar (Imray)
63 routes with full passage tables.
An indispensable companion for planning Thames estuary passages, this set of tables enables navigators to select the best routes according to tide times.

Chart packs (paper and digital)
2000 Suffolk and Essex coasts
2100 Kent and Sussex coasts

Planning charts
C1	Thames Estuary	1:120,000
C2	The River Thames	Various
Y6	Suffolk and Essex Coasts	1:120,000
Y12	Rivers Stour and Orwell	Various

Harbour charts
Y2	Rivers Ore and Alde	1:35,000
Y16	Walton Backwaters to Ipswich and Woodbridge	1:35,000
Y17	The Rivers Colne, Blackwater, Crouch and Roach	1:50,000
Y18	The River Medway and approaches	1:20,000
Y14	The Swale	1:40,000

Imray Digital
ID10 North Sea

Rites of Passage **31**

Across the Bristol Channel

Jane Cumberlidge

PENZANCE TO MILFORD HAVEN VIA LUNDY

Rounding Land's End for the first time is an exciting prospect and crossing the Bristol Channel to Wales looks like real exploration when you study the charts and tidal atlas. I was about to experience both these rites of passage and was enjoying being in Cornwall as we prepared to set off towards Milford Haven.

We'd spent three relaxing days in Penzance doing a few jobs on board our gaff cutter *Stormalong* and getting to know the town. There are plenty of salty old pubs and I'd visited Penlee House, a superb museum and gallery of the Newlyn School of Art.

Land's End is a serious headland, and beyond it the Bristol Channel has a daunting reputation, partly because of its big tides but also because the wild and rugged coasts have fewer bolt-holes and marinas than we are used to on the south coast. In open water, even a moderate wind-over-tide kicks up short, steep seas in the Bristol Channel, while along the coasts overfalls can be savage off the main headlands.

The 100-mile direct passage from Land's End to Milford Haven runs at an angle to the Bristol Channel streams, but can leave you exposed to weather changes.

We'd planned our passage in gentle tidal stages – Penzance to St Ives, up the Cornish coast to Padstow, then a hop to Lundy Island before crossing to Milford Haven. Each leg was about 35 miles long, a pleasant day sail for *Stormalong* in the friendly conditions that had been forecast. We'd also chosen a period around neap tides.

Our departure day was perfect and in warm sunshine we carried a light easterly down the glorious expanse of Mount's Bay, catching the southerly ebb to be at the Runnel Stone buoy about an hour before HW Dover. Mousehole looked pretty in the morning light and soon beautiful Porthcurno beach opened up, with the Minack Theatre on its cliff top.

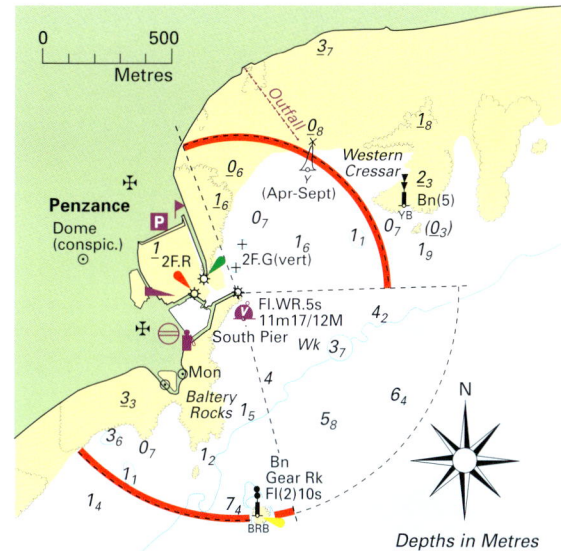

Keeping outside the Runnel Stone, we curved north-west past Gwennap Head and brought Land's End fine on the starboard bow. The sea was quiet with hardly any swell. Up on the headland, crowds gazed out towards Longships Lighthouse. We were using the scenic inshore passage and I needed to identify Kettle's Bottom, the nasty eastern outlier of the Longships reef. Suddenly the gap seemed horribly narrow but *Stormalong*'s steady motion calmed my nerves. Her long keel and big gaff mainsail mean she isn't at all flighty and, once in the groove, holds her course.

We were using the early fair tide running inshore. Sennen Cove opened to starboard as we crossed Whitesand Bay and passed the two humps of the Brisons. Here was my first cape, Cape Cornwall, topped by the stark chimney of a tin mine. Passing Pendeen Head, its overfalls lazy today, we hardened up towards St Ives, the tide still fair on this conveniently timed run which can give you an 8-hour window for entering the Bristol Channel in this direction.

Far left
Lundy southeast landing
Peter Cumberlidge

Below
Penzance Dock
Peter Cumberlidge

Rites of Passage **33**

4 ACROSS THE BRISTOL CHANNEL

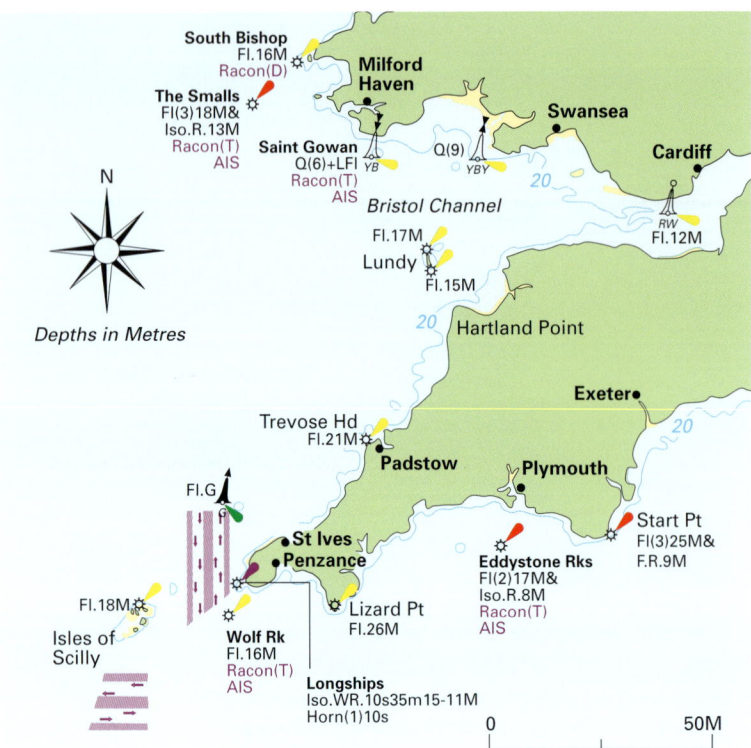

PASSAGE PLANNER
Departure from Penzance

Standard Port Plymouth

HWS	−0108	HWN	−0053
LWS	−0035	LWN	−0036

MHWS	MHWN	MLWN	MLWS
0·0m	−0·1m	−0·2m	0·0m

A passage round Land's End needs reliably settled weather. Penzance is a good jumping off point and well placed for timing the tides. Passing the Runnel Stone two hours before HW Dover, you can carry at least eight hours of north and then north-east-going fair stream into the Bristol Channel. For a quieter life, we chose a period with the tide falling off towards neaps.

Sailing the 115M direct from Penzance to Milford Haven means crossing the Bristol Channel overnight and a staged passage via Padstow is more pleasant and interesting. From Padstow to Milford Haven is only 68M. Leaving Padstow when the gate opens, two hours before HW at springs, you'll have a moderate NE-going set off Cornwall to start with. The direct track passes 15M west of Lundy and on the Welsh side about 6M west of St Gowan Shoals S-cardinal buoy. Off the Pembrokeshire coast the west-going stream will be gathering pace, so aim to make landfall close to Linney Head, to stay safely east of the Turbot Bank. You can enter the Haven by the East or West channels, though the East is more direct on this approach.

Tacking round St Ives Head, we anchored south-east of the breakwater, with views across to a golden beach and along to Godrevy Island. In the light easterlies the bay was sheltered and we spent a peaceful night.

Next morning the wind had slipped south of east and freshened a touch, giving a useful slant across St Ives Bay and through The Sound between The Stones and Godrevy. *Stormalong* was now sailing up the 'shipwreck coast', the legendary lee shore that has trapped so many vessels down through the centuries. The fluky breeze off the looming cliffs made us glad of the full tide for the 30 miles to Padstow, though you definitely want too little rather than too much wind along here.

Stormalong at sea
David Lomax

It was fun passing the famous surfing beaches at Perranporth and Newquay. The occasional ruined chimney or old brick building showed that this stretch of the Cornish coast was once a busy industrial area in the 18th and 19th centuries. Wrecking and smuggling were also nice little earners.

The breeze finally died under the cliffs and we motored on in a glassy calm. Our deadline at the mouth of the River Camel was just before high water Padstow, to allow a safe crossing of Doom Bar and then entering the wet basin. Approaching Trevose Head across Watergate Bay, we left Quies Rocks to starboard, passed inside Gulland Rock and then skirted Stepper Point. The entrance channel follows the east side of the outer estuary past Trebetherick Point, but then hugs the west shore on the final approach to Padstow basin. Settled at a cosy quayside berth, we just made it to our favourite Italian restaurant for a late supper.

I'd lived in Barnstaple many years ago but never managed to visit Lundy, so now was my chance. The light southeasterlies stayed with us the next day and we reached north-northeast

34 Rites of Passage

PENZANCE TO MILFORD HAVEN VIA LUNDY

towards Hartland Point, staying within a mile of the coast once the tide turned foul. We passed Tintagel, Boscastle and Bude, all evocative names in Cornish history and folklore. From a distance Lundy looked like a huge ship out in the roads. It was quiet enough to anchor off Lundy's southeast corner near the ferry jetty. With the hook well dug in, we sculled ashore for a climb to the top. The weather was clear with magnificent views across Barnstaple Bay to Hartland Point, Baggy Point and Bull Point. We called at the Marisco Tavern to sample their local ale – only a swift half as we were edgy about leaving *Stormalong* alone too long.

Our Welsh landfall was to be Linney Head, a few miles south-east of Milford Haven entrance. The direct track from Lundy is north-northwest and we planned to leave St Gowan Shoals and cardinal buoy to starboard, make for Linney and follow the coast towards Sheep Island, with the Turbot Bank safely to the southwest.

I'd sailed off Brittany's northwest corner before, but somehow the Bristol Channel feels more remote and exposed. On a fine summer day though, North Devon and southwest Wales make spectacular departures and arrivals, and the Channel has a grandeur we were lucky to experience in kind conditions. Our easterly had

St Ives Bay and Godrevy Island
Peter Cumberlidge

Padstow Harbour
Peter Cumberlidge

Rites of Passage **35**

4 ACROSS THE BRISTOL CHANNEL

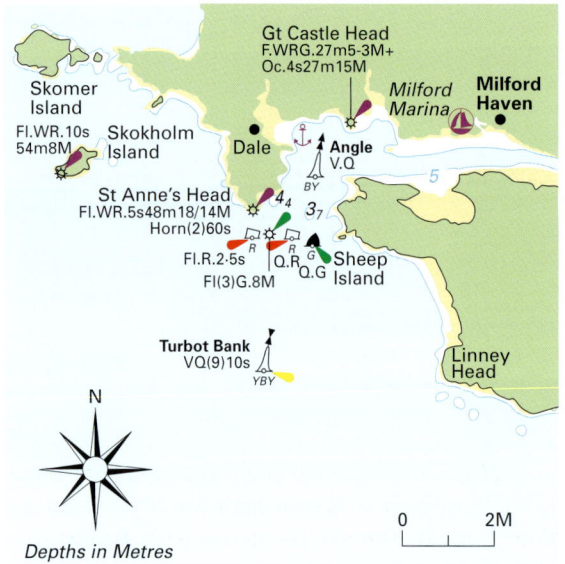

Arrival at Milford Haven

Standard Port Milford Haven

Milford Haven is a reliable port of refuge, providing all tide, all weather access. Entry is straightforward, day or night, though streams in and out of the Haven can cause confused seas where they meet the main Bristol Channel flow.

On the west side of the entrance, St Ann's Head lighthouse (Fl.WR.5s.48m18/14M) is visible. Enter the West Channel between St Ann's port hand buoy and Mid Channel Rocks W cardinal, then continue at 040°T towards Great Castle Head (F.WRG.27m5/3/3M) as far as Angle N cardinal buoy. The East channel starts half a mile WSW of Sheep Island, leaving Sheep starboard hand buoy close to starboard.

stiffened a little, driving us from the Lundy anchorage a bit early, but giving a cracking reach over a sparkling sea.

The Pembrokeshire coast looked stunning, especially the limestone cliffs and ancient weathered stacks between Linney and Saint Govan's Heads. Entering Milford Haven by the east channel, we watched seals lolling about on Sheep Island. With the wind forecast to veer south-westerly overnight, we headed towards Dale, just inside the Haven on the west side, and anchored off Musselwick Point. There's a very old pub in Dale village, the Griffin Inn, and here we savoured delicious Cwrw Haf Welsh blond ale and homemade fish pie to celebrate our arrival in Wales.

The seasonal visitors' pontoon at Dale
Peter Cumberlidge

WHY VISIT MILFORD HAVEN?

Milford Haven is one of the most attractive and fascinating cruising estuaries in Britain. Geologically it is a sunken, deep water ria, with the Cleddau River winding 22 miles inland from St Ann's Head up to Haverfordwest. Lord Nelson thought it one of the best natural harbours in the world and Shakespeare used it for a scene in Cymbeline. This grand, perfectly sheltered roadstead was also used by the Romans and the Vikings. Henry Tudor was born here in Pembroke Castle and Oliver Cromwell set off from the Haven to invade Ireland. In the late 1800s, Milford was one of Britain's most important fishing ports and in the 1930s the RAF

36 Rites of Passage

Milford Haven Wattick Bay
Peter Cumberlidge

had a flying-boat base at Pembroke Dock. Atlantic convoys assembled here during WWII.

Milford Haven developed as an oil port from the late 1950s but there was a major decline in activity by the 1990s. Over the last ten years a couple of refineries have been recommissioned or repurposed. Despite this renewed tanker activity the Haven still has plenty of room for pleasurable leisure activity afloat.

There are two good marinas in the Haven, Milford Marina in the town dock and Neyland Yacht Haven in a quiet creek about four miles further up, almost opposite Pembroke Dock which is active with Irish ferries. There are numerous places to anchor and Dale has a seasonal visitors' pontoon.

Beyond the Cleddau road bridge most yachts can reach Lawrenny Quay, an attractive retreat for a night or two. Above Lawrenny depths start reducing, though the upper reaches have some interesting anchorages. One of my favourite hideaways is opposite Benton Castle, whose white tower rises above the surrounding oak trees. Further up you can anchor off Llangwm Pill. At Picton Point the river divides into the East and West Cleddau. You might find a vacant buoy in the East river, and near high water you can take a dinghy three miles up the West arm to Haverfordwest.

The wide lower reaches of the Haven have many possible anchorages, with glorious sandy beaches to tempt you ashore and secret creeks for shallow draft boats that can take the ground. Just east of Dale, Sandy Haven is a charming wooded creek where bilge-keelers can hide away from the world. On the south side of the Haven, Angle Bay is a wide shallow inlet, useful in winds from the south or southeast.

From the shelter of Milford Haven it's easy to plan a day sail out to Skokholm and Skomer islands. Both are run by the Wildlife Trust of South and West Wales and are internationally important bird sanctuaries. Passing through Jack Sound, between Skomer and the mainland, you reach North Haven anchorage where you can land on the island. Be sure to contact the warden here, either by VHF before you land or by calling at his bungalow, to pay your landing fee which helps with the upkeep of this magical place.

Neyland Marina
Peter Cumberlidge

4 ACROSS THE BRISTOL CHANNEL

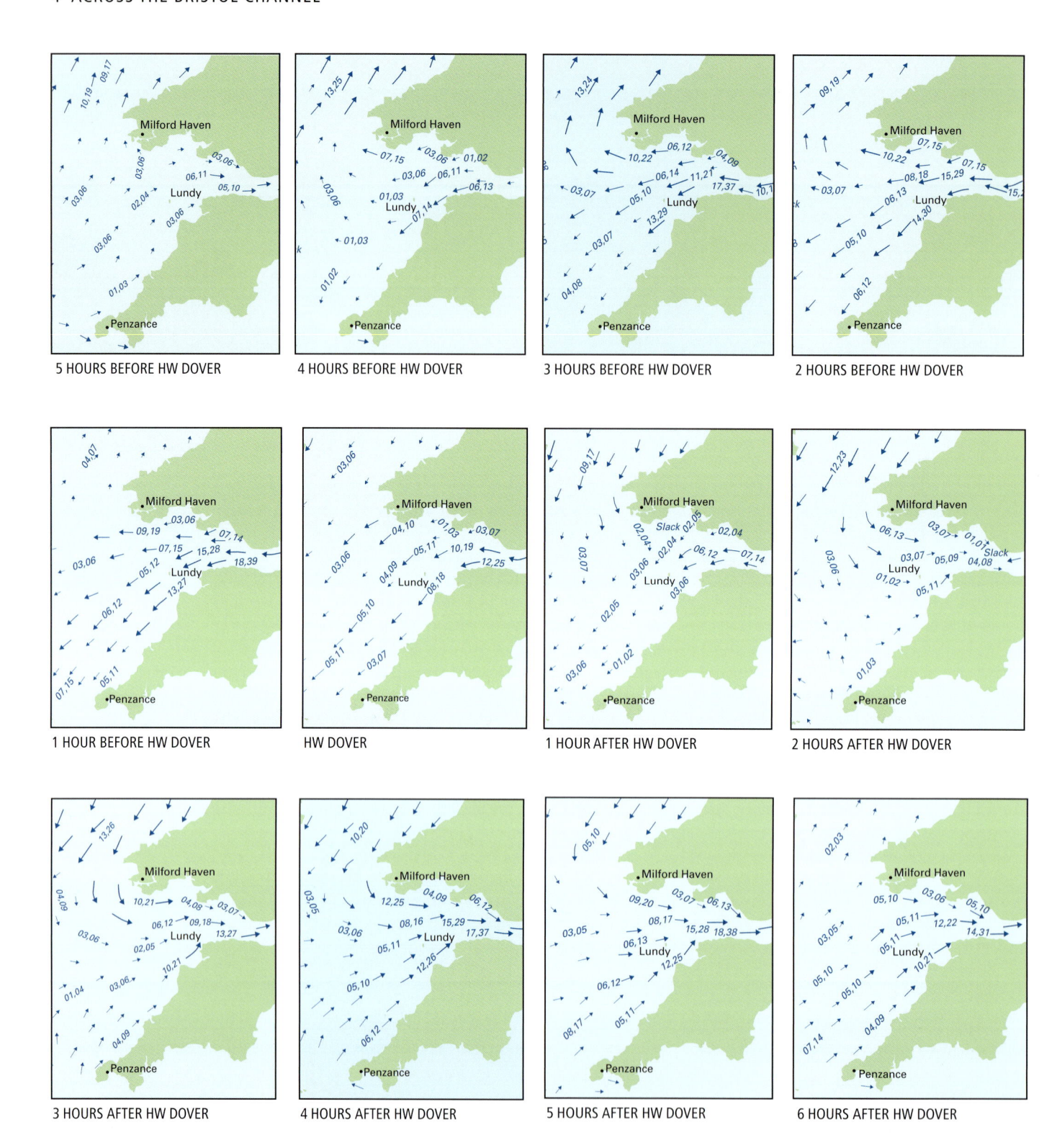

5 HOURS BEFORE HW DOVER

4 HOURS BEFORE HW DOVER

3 HOURS BEFORE HW DOVER

2 HOURS BEFORE HW DOVER

1 HOUR BEFORE HW DOVER

HW DOVER

1 HOUR AFTER HW DOVER

2 HOURS AFTER HW DOVER

3 HOURS AFTER HW DOVER

4 HOURS AFTER HW DOVER

5 HOURS AFTER HW DOVER

6 HOURS AFTER HW DOVER

TIDAL STREAMS

The figures shown against the arrows are the mean rates at neaps and springs in tenths of a knot. Thus 07,15 - mean neaps rate 0·7 knots, mean springs rate 1·5 knots

IMRAY TIDES PLANNER

Imray Tides Planner app is a useful planning tool. Download from the App Store or Google Play.

38 Rites of Passage

Skomer Island
Peter Cumberlidge

About the author

JANE CUMBERLIDGE started sailing as an undergraduate when she cruised to the Baltic with her sister and brother-in-law aboard a converted lifeboat. Later she cruised widely with her husband Peter aboard *Stormalong*, their 1936 gaff cutter. The Cumberlidges lived in Wales for many years, when Jane first sailed around Land's End to discover Bristol Channel waters. Jane is also a specialist on inland waterways boating in Britain, Ireland and France. She is a regular contributor for Waterways World magazine and her books are published by Imray.

Imray books and charts

Bristol Channel and River Severn Cruising Guide
Peter Cumberlidge (Imray)

With an authoritative and highly readable tone this covers nearly every creek, pill, river and harbour from Milford Haven to St Ives via Lydney and Bristol, including the fixed-mast canal route from Sharpness to Gloucester. It is beautifully illustrated throughout, with a comprehensive set of harbour chartlets.

The West Country
Carlos Rojas and Susan Kemp-Wheeler (Imray)

Covering Lyme Bay to Land's End and the Isles of Scilly it provides essential sailing directions and detailed listings of facilities together with a wealth of information for those wishing to learn about the West Country and enjoy trips ashore.

Chart packs (paper and digital)
2400 West Country
2600 Bristol Channel

Planning charts
C7	Falmouth to Isles of Scilly and Trevose Head	1:120 000
C58	Trevose Head to Bull Point	1:130,000
C60	Gower Peninsula to Cardigan	1:130,000

Harbour charts
Y26	Milford Haven and River Cleddau	1:30/25 000
	Milford Marina	1:15 000
	Neyland Yacht Haven	1:10 000

Imray Digital
ID30 West Britain and Ireland

Across the North Channel

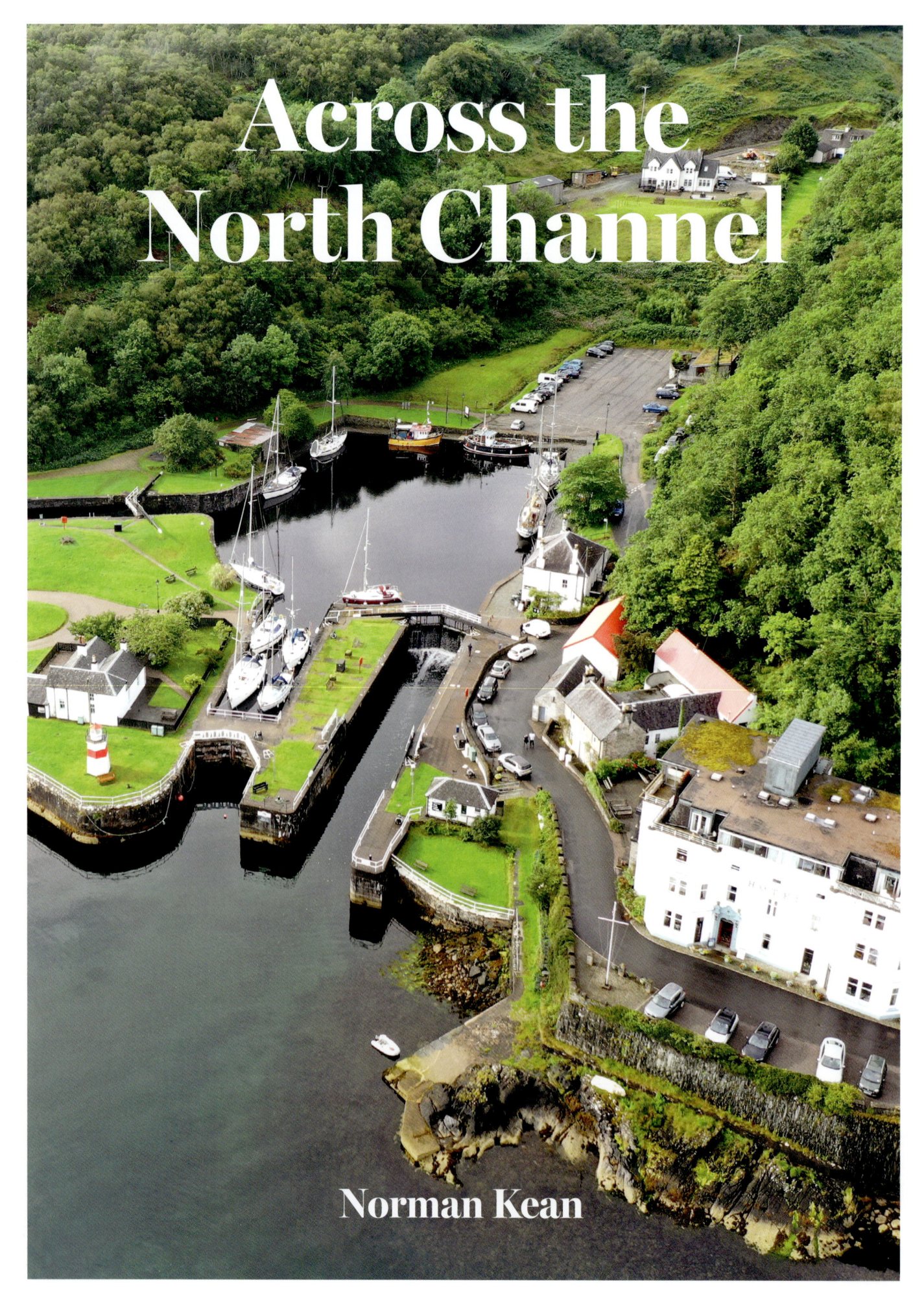

Norman Kean

We were alongside in Crinan basin, surely one of the most picturesque places in the world. The nine-mile Crinan Canal, built before the days of steam to bypass the steep seas and fast tides of the Mull of Kintyre, is a pure gem. It's almost possible to get from here to the north coast of Ireland, over 50M, in one tide, but we weren't in a hurry as there are many lovely anchorages in between. The tide would turn south at 1000, and five or six hours would take us to Islay or Gigha and halfway to Ireland. We were following an ancient sea-lane. In 700AD this was the heart of the kingdom of Dalriada, stretching from Mull to Ulster and with its capital here at Dunadd on Loch Crinan.

The sea-lock gates swung open, our lines were dropped to the deck and we motored slowly out into the loch. As we cleared the crenellated sea wall below the hotel, the magnificent panorama of the islands to the northwest opened up. Garbh Reisa and the Dorus Mor, with Reisa an t-Sruith beyond, and looming over them the grey-green bulk of Scarba. Just closed in by the north end of Jura was the Gulf of Corryvreckan, where the fast tides of this sea are at their most dangerous. But we were headed the other way. The forecast was for moderate west to northwest winds – a close reach, with luck – and flat seas. The Sound of Jura has tides that can reach three-and-a-half knots at springs, but it was coming on neaps, and we could expect a push of a knot or two at the most.

With all plain sail pulling nicely we were off Carsaig Bay within the hour. Here a narrow neck of land separates the Sound from Loch Sween, with the village of Tayvallich on its bay on the loch. These days you'll usually hear it pronounced as it's written, but I remember when you'd be corrected. It's Tay-vyallich, showing its Gaelic origin as Tigh a'Bhealaich — the house on the pass. Three miles across the Sound, the almost deserted north end of Jura, a Norse name this time, dyr-øy — the island of deer, where they still outnumber the humans by forty-to-one. It was in a remote farmhouse at this end of Jura in 1948 that George Orwell, already dying of tuberculosis, wrote *Nineteen Eighty-Four*.

We had a choice to make for an overnight stop at Gigha to the east, or Islay to the west. Gigha has many attractions, not least of them the hotel, and visitors' moorings, but we opted to hold on to our distance to windward with a forecast of a backing wind. So Islay it was. Its southeast corner is a little jumble of islets, the Ardmore Islands and behind them is a really special anchorage.

Dominating the skyline to the south-west, the quartzite scree of the Paps of Jura was glittering in the sun as the light-tower on Skervuile drew closer, and the buildings of Craighouse, Jura's only township, peeped out between the islets sheltering its bay. A stack of logs on the pier was evidence of the busy trade in timber from the forests of Argyll — spruce and larch planted after the Second World War, now mature and being felled, much of it for shipment to Ireland. The breeze stiffened out of the Sound of Islay as we cleared the south end of Jura, and we eased sheets briefly in good time, to pass astern of the ferry *Finlaggan*, on her twice-daily run to Port Askaig.

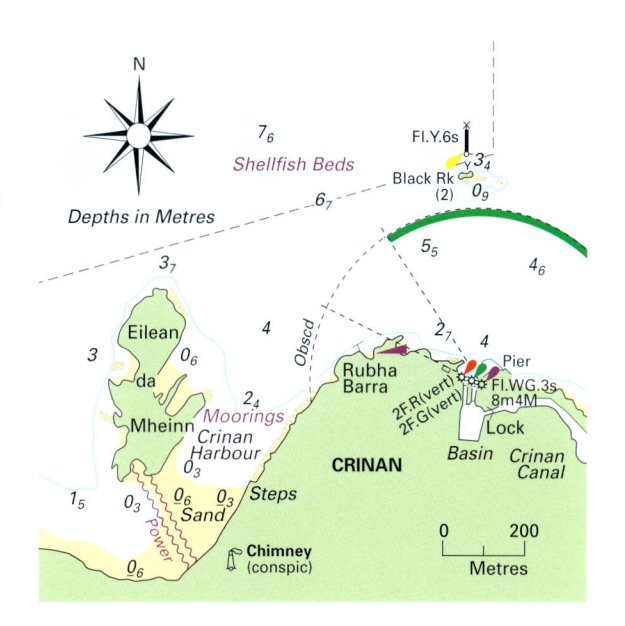

We could just make out the little beacon on Eilean a'Chuirn, the easternmost of the Ardmore Islands, and we set our course for Caolas Port na Lice, the short cut into our anchorage from the east. The channel is described by the Clyde Cruising Club as 'canal-like'. It's half a mile long and half a cable wide between the rocky shore and above-water reefs. The bay where it opens out would make a passable anchorage, but tucked away behind a string of islets and reefs just here is Plod Sgeirean: 'very remote and inaccessible, and teeming with wildlife'.

Opposite Crinan
Norman Kean

Below Crinan
Mike Bamforth

5 ACROSS THE NORTH CHANNEL

PASSAGE PLANNER

Crinan Canal

The canal runs across the base of the Kintyre Peninsula to Ardrishaig on Loch Fyne thus saving a sometimes difficult 80M passage round the Mull to the Clyde. The Canal is 9M long with 15 locks and seven swing bridges and can take vessels up to 26·8m LOA, 6m beam and 2·7m draught in fresh water. Note: you should add 100mm to your sea water draught to get fresh water draught. www.scottishcanals.co.uk.

Departure from Crinan

Standard Port Oban

HWS	–0025	HWN	–0055
LWS	–0040	LWN	+0035

MHWS	MHWN	MLWN	MLWS
–1·2m	–0·8m	–0·5m	–0·1m

The Sound of Jura is best taken with the south-going tide, which starts at HW Oban –0110. The shores of the Sound are generally clean and the rocks Skervuile and Na Cuiltean are both marked by lit beacons. There are many anchorages: on the east side Carsaig Bay, Eilean Mor MacCormaig, Loch Sween, Loch Caolisport, and lovely bays on Gigha, while to the west are Lowlandman's Bay and Craighouse on Jura. Few places in the world have such a varied abundance of anchorages as the west coast of Scotland.

The crossing to Ireland can be made at any state of the tide, given due allowance, but particularly if headed further south it makes sense to take the east- and south-going flood, which starts at HW Oban –0030. Other landfalls in Ireland include Ballycastle, south of Rathlin, Portrush to the west, and Glenarm on the east Antrim coast. Tides on that coast reach 4 knots at springs but there are no difficult headlands. Mention of fog in weather forecasts should be taken seriously as Rathlin and the North Channel are prone to it.

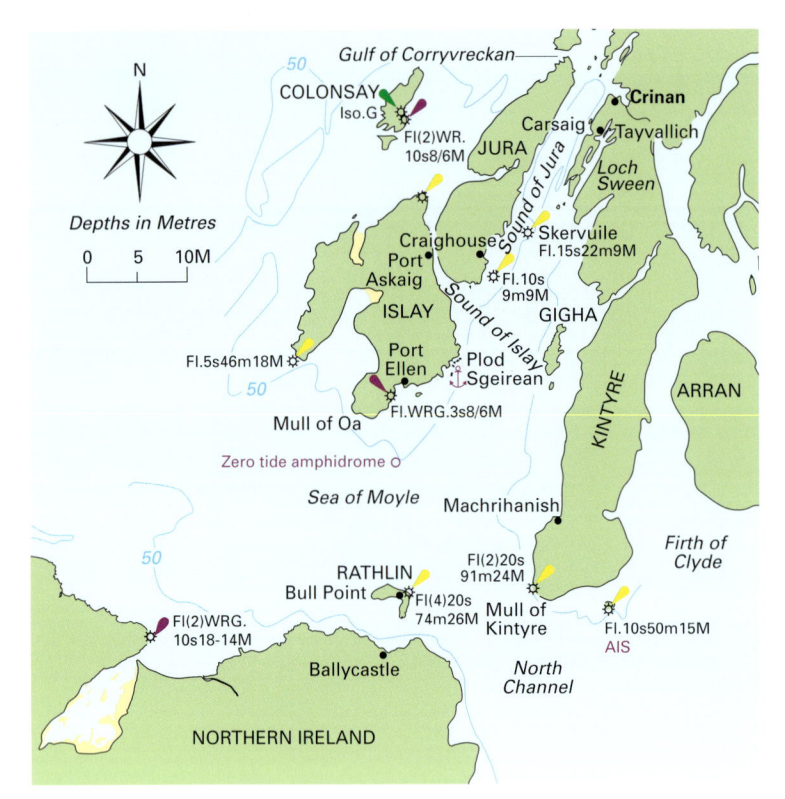

Our anchor splashed into four metres of clear water, and we gave it a good heave astern for fear of kelp. This is a place where virtually no allowance is needed for the rise and fall of the tide, because it's only a few inches at neaps. There's an odd tidal phenomenon south of Islay, called an amphidrome, where the tidal range is zero. Its effects are felt as far north as Corryvreckan – indeed it could be said that, paradoxically, it's the reason for Corryvreckan – and on much of the Irish coast as well.

Plod Sgeirean has a tranquillity all of its own. The chances are you'd have it to yourself, as we did. This is off the beaten track, since most people turn north out of Crinan. It's a mile or two off the nearest road, too, single track with passing places and petering out three miles on. The curious seals swim right up to the boat, and a fearless otter darted to and fro under our dinghy, oblivious to the outboard propeller as we explored the shore.

A curious seal at Plod Sgeirean
Geraldine Hennigan

42 Rites of Passage

Plod Sgeirean
Norman Kean

Then he was off into the kelp in pursuit of a tasty crab for dinner.

Next morning dawned fine and fair. The wind had slackened and backed only as far as west. Allowing for the south-east-going flood tide meant a beat, but a pleasant one.

Once clear of the Ardmore Islands, the coast of Ireland was laid out before us, stretching over 60 degrees of the compass: the plateau and black basalt cliffs of Rathlin 20 miles to the south, with the broad hump of Knocklayd behind; the mainland cliffs of Antrim and Derry straggling west to the distinctive escarpment of Binevenagh; and faint in the haze to the south-west, the peak of Slieve Snaght in Donegal. Beyond Rathlin to the east, there are the high cliffs of Fair Head, and behind Gigha the green hills of Kintyre, which climb beyond Machrihanish to high moorland falling abruptly to the sea at the Mull. The mountains of Arran towered blue beyond Kintyre. Visibility here can reach 70 miles on a good day.

We began to feel the ocean swell as we came out of the lee of the Mull of Oa to the west. An occasional swirl betrayed the eastward-streaming tide, and our course over ground showed that we were making 15 degrees leeway in the current. There's a traffic scheme north of Rathlin but getting through it is never a problem as the traffic is light.

Today there was just one ship on the horizon, heading east, a laden tanker bound for Milford Haven from the Shetland oil terminal. Rathlin was distinct now from the background cliffs, with the upside-down Bull Point lighthouse at its western tip. Rafts of puffins greeted us as we swept past the point and eased sheets for the short run in to the harbour. Before the breakwaters were built, the road up past the pub provided the

Seal pups
Geraldine Hennigan

Rites of Passage

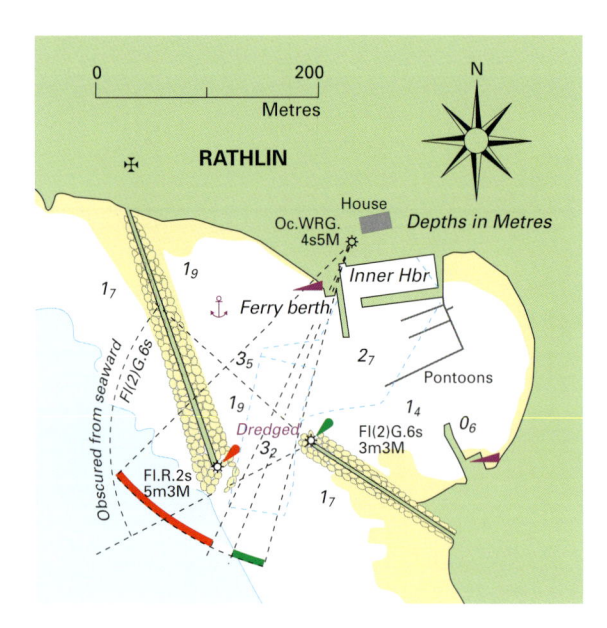

5 ACROSS THE NORTH CHANNEL

Arrival at Rathlin Island

Standard Port Belfast

| HWS | −0450 | HWN | −0155 |
| LWS | −0452 | LWN | −0136 |

| MHWS | MHWN | MLWN | MLWS |
| −2·2m | −2·0m | −0·4m | 0·0m |

The tide in Rathlin Sound can reach 6 knots, with overfalls in wind-over-tide conditions, but in the crook of the island the streams are slacker, and Bull Point is perhaps the least challenging of the island's three corners. The harbour at Church Bay is protected by two rubble breakwaters, lit at night and enclosing a basin a cable each way and two to four metres deep. A directional light also marks the approach from the SW. Strong winds from W or NW can cause the entrance to break right across, particularly during the last two hours of the east-going tide. There is pontoon berthing in the harbour for at least 20 visiting yachts. Local craft are confined to small RIBs and inshore fishing boats. Two ferryboats sail to Ballycastle.

leading line over the rock bar known as The Bow. It still says McCuaig's Bar in big white letters on the roof, and it was beckoning. We were in Ireland now. The welcome pint would have to be Guinness.

WHY VISIT RATHLIN?

Rathlin is in Northern Ireland, yet - in a way - not of it. None of the province's stereotypes apply here - the challenges and freedoms of life on a small island, cut off by three miles of sluicing tide, outweigh all else for its community of 150. It's a thriving place, in contrast to forty years ago, when there was no proper harbour, no mains electricity, and the population was 75 and falling. The island was revived steadily from the 1980s by harbour development and improved ferry services, and a renewed sense of enterprise. The focus is on tourism - the island is home to tens of thousands of seabirds, most notably puffins but also black guillemots, razorbills and kittiwakes. The RSPB's Seabird Centre at Bull Point attracts tens of thousands of visitors each year.

Marine fauna are equally plentiful - this is a hot spot for grey seals, whales, dolphins and basking sharks. Rathlin's north coast has many underwater caves, which are home to 130 species of sponges, anemones and hydroids, as well as

Bull Point, Rathlin
Geraldine Hennigan

44 Rites of Passage

Rathlin Harbour
Norman Kean

lobsters and crabs. The waters around the island are one of Northern Ireland's three Marine Conservation Zones. There are many wrecks nearby, the biggest of them the 14,000-ton armoured cruiser Drake, which capsized and sank in Church Bay after being torpedoed in 1917. The wreck, with 8m of water over it, is marked by a south cardinal buoy. McCuaig's Bar is decorated with salvaged items from this and many other wrecks.

The coastal scenery and the views are spectacular – from the 70-metre clifftops the Mull of Kintyre seems only a stone's throw away. The island offers beautiful walks, there are bikes for hire, and McCuaig's Bar, the Manor House Restaurant, and the Water Shed Cafe offer food to suit all tastes.

The geology of the island is unusual. The basalt plateau lies on top of chalk, visible as a white band in the cliffs on the south side. The pebbles on the beach form a chequerboard of black and white. In Neolithic times, between 6,000 and 4,500 years ago, there was a stone axe factory on the island, using a rock called porcellanite. Rathlin is one of only two Irish locations where this material occurs, and it evidently exported its axes all over Ireland.

Legend has it that about 1305, having suffered many setbacks in his guerilla war against the English, the Scottish leader Robert Bruce was in hiding in a cave on Rathlin. There he was inspired by a doggedly persistent web-building spider to have one more attempt, a course that was to be crowned with success when, as King Robert of Scotland, he led his armies to victory at Bannockburn in 1314. Sadly the spider story is probably a myth, but it's a good one nevertheless, and Bruce's (reputed) Cave is one of Rathlin's tourist attractions.

There's no myth, however, about the connection between the island and the invention of radio. In 1898 Guglielmo Marconi set up the world's first commercial wireless telegraphy link between here and Ballycastle. The Irish association is no coincidence. You can celebrate it with a glass or two – Marconi's grandfather was the whiskey distiller Andrew Jameson.

Coire Uisge, the author's yacht
Inge Leth-Olsen

Rites of Passage **45**

5 ACROSS THE NORTH CHANNEL

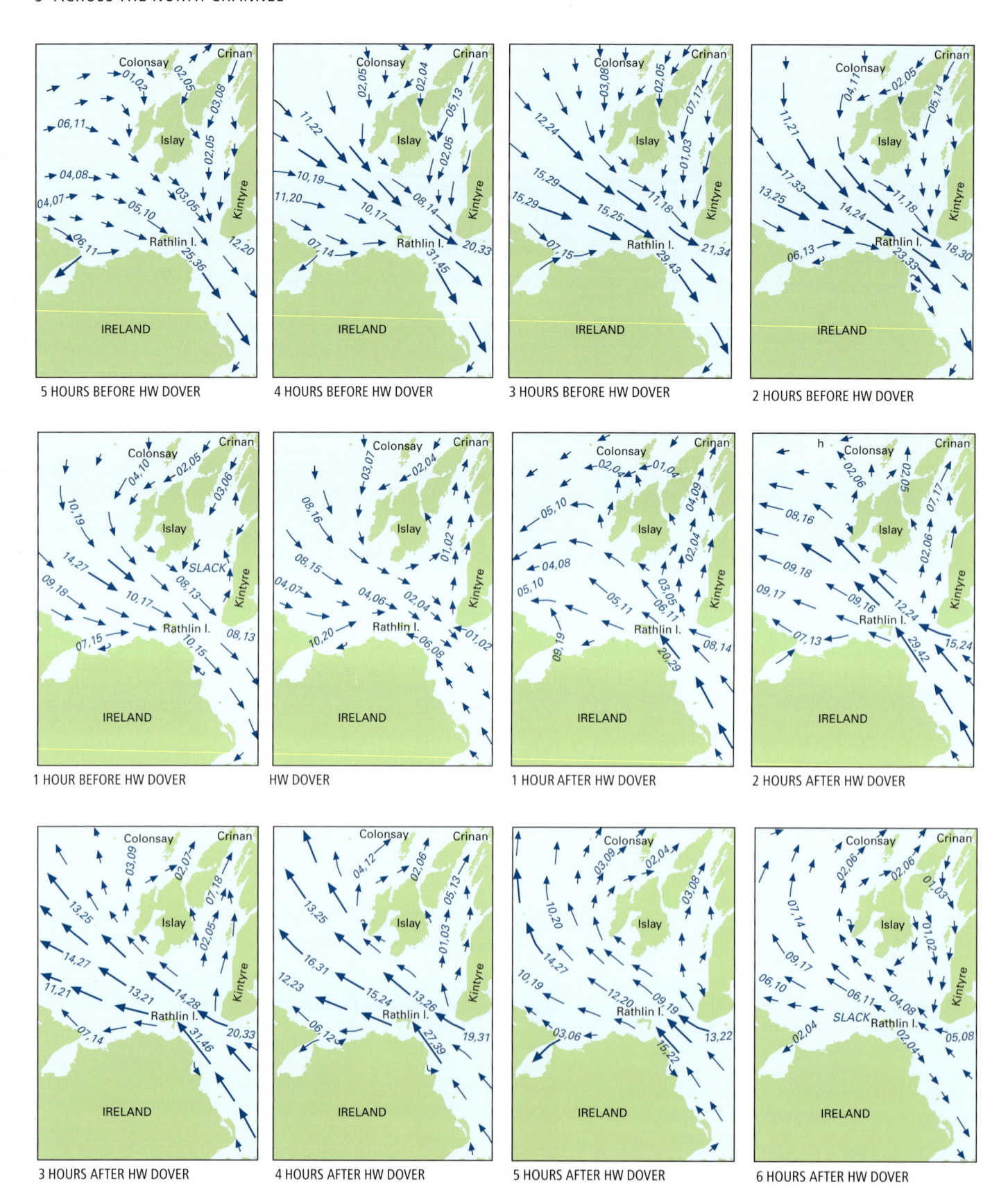

5 HOURS BEFORE HW DOVER

4 HOURS BEFORE HW DOVER

3 HOURS BEFORE HW DOVER

2 HOURS BEFORE HW DOVER

1 HOUR BEFORE HW DOVER

HW DOVER

1 HOUR AFTER HW DOVER

2 HOURS AFTER HW DOVER

3 HOURS AFTER HW DOVER

4 HOURS AFTER HW DOVER

5 HOURS AFTER HW DOVER

6 HOURS AFTER HW DOVER

TIDAL STREAMS

The figures shown against the arrows are the mean rates at neaps and springs in tenths of a knot. Thus 07,15 - mean neaps rate 0·7 knots, mean springs rate 1·5 knots

IMRAY TIDES PLANNER

Imray Tides Planner app is a useful planning tool. Download from the App Store or Google Play.

Nesting fulmars on the cliffs of Bull Point, seen from the RSPB lookout
Geraldine Hennigan

About the author

NORMAN KEAN is a native of Argyll who spent many summers cruising the west coast of Scotland. He lived in Northern Ireland for 17 years and has been editor of the Irish Cruising Club's Sailing Directions since 2005. He and his wife Geraldine Hennigan now sail their Warrior 40 *Coire Uisge* from their home base in Courtmacsherry, County Cork. Norman is a Yachtmaster (Offshore) and a Fellow of the Royal Institute of Navigation. In 2012, he co-authored *Cruising Ireland*, with the late Mike Balmforth.

Imray books and charts

Kintyre to Ardnamurchan
Clyde Cruising Club (Imray)
The best pilotage that is available for the west of the Kintyre peninsula, Islay, Jura, Mull, the Small Isles, and adjacent coasts north to Fort William and Ardnamurchan.

East and North Coast of Ireland
(Irish Cruising Club Publications)
Covering Kilmore Quay and Carnsore Point, northward via Malin Head to the Bloody Foreland. This 13th edition includes new information from a comprehensive revisiting of the coast. With 99 aerial and 294 sea-level photographs, 99 plans and updated marina information in a new easier-to-use format.

Chart packs (paper and digital)
2800 Kintyre to Ardnamurchan
2900 Firth of Clyde

Planning chart
C64 North Channel   1:160 000

Imray Digital
ID30 West Britain and Ireland

Across the English Channel

Ros Hogbin

HAMBLE TO BRAYE

In the years before children, we took the fast-track approach to Channel crossing: up before dawn, swerve round the Isle of Wight, look left – dodge ships, look right – dodge ships; face the inevitable southwesterly and tumble into Braye Harbour, determined to be ashore before closing time.

When our three boys were very small, we opted for the line of least resistance: get them into their bunks by 1900 and get as far as you can overnight. Keep them in their bunks as long as is humanly possible next morning and plough on. Arrive when the sun's high, completely shattered; and let them shriek 'Beach, beach!' at you 'til you give in and launch the dinghy.

Several years of Mediterranean sailing later, we were eager to revisit Alderney, this time with the help of our boys, now aged 12 to 17. We were between boats, so we found a little charter company online and booked a Beneteau Oceanis 37 for the trip.

Crossing the English Channel is a significant undertaking – however and whenever you do it. Weather, tides, average boat speed and very busy shipping lanes all need to be considered. We cleared the dining room table and dusted down our dog-eared tidal stream atlases. Our elder two set to work with dividers and tide tables. How far are we going? If it takes us 12 hours to cross, does that mean the tides cancel out? What happens if it takes 18 hours? When do we want to arrive? Woah! Look at the tides round Alderney! Our youngest opened the new edition of *The Channel Islands, Cherbourg Peninsula and North Brittany* pilot (Imray) and chipped in with comments about the Alderney lighthouse and beach games in Longy Bay. Well remembered! He'd last been there when he was four.

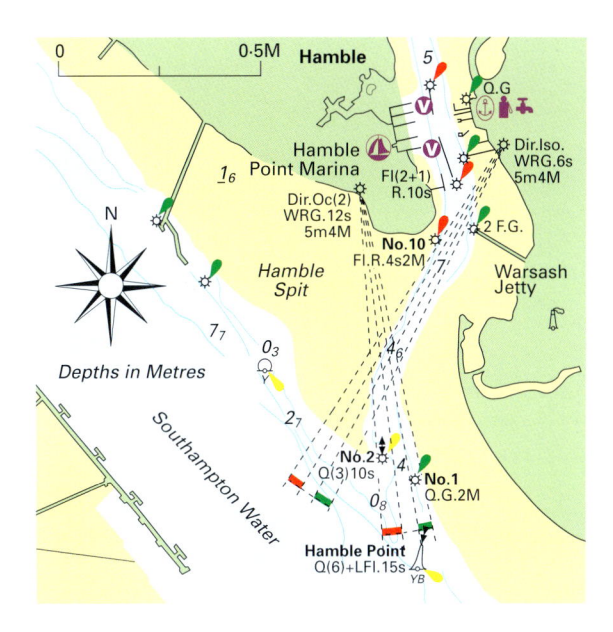

Charter handover completed, we discussed departure time. Tomorrow looked good. Wind nudging just north of west for most of the day, but back to the southwest after that and no let up. We decided to grab the opportunity. By 0930 next morning we had safely left the marina and motored down the Hamble river. Which way now? South west towards the Needles would give us a better crossing angle and shorter distance to Alderney. However, with wind and tide against us all morning, we'd be bashing to get to the Needles Channel before the tide turned.

If we missed that gate, we'd be at the mercy of strong wind over spring tide in a nasty patch of water. Alternatively, we could go with the tide down the east side of the island past Bembridge. Then, as the tide turned, we would head south and out across the Channel. We opted for the latter.

Passage planning gets everyone involved
Ros Hogbin

Far left
Longy Bay, Alderney - perfect for beach games
Visit Alderney

Rites of Passage **49**

6 ACROSS THE ENGLISH CHANNEL

PASSAGE PLANNER
Departure from River Hamble

Standard Port Southampton

Warsash

HWS	−0010	HWN	+0020
LWS	0000	LWN	−0010
MHWS	MHWN	MLWN	MLWS
0.0m	+0·1m	−0·1m	+0·3m

It's 60M from The Needles to Braye or 73M from Nab Tower, so a 10+ hour passage. Find a window of settled weather. Depending on your speed, the Channel tidal streams may set you unequally E and W of your track, so adjust your planned heading to offset any E-W imbalance. Alderney sits within ferocious E-W tidal streams; check the tidal atlas and time your arrival to coincide with local slack water. Exiting the Solent via the Needles offers a shorter crossing, but if faced with strong wind over tide, it may pay to head down the east of the Isle of Wight. Once clear of St Catherine's Point, even a straight-line heading becomes a diverse track, set high and low by wind angle and changing tidal stream. Avoid the charted Traffic Separation Scheme (TSS) but you will still be crossing busy lanes. Use radar and AIS if you have them and keep a good lookout.

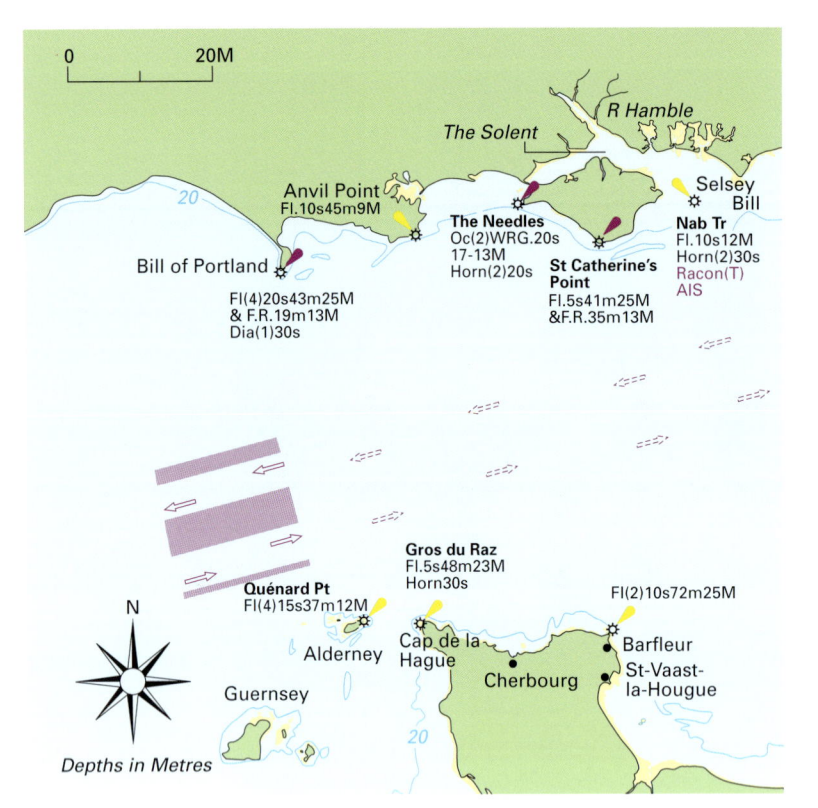

The boat handled beautifully as we sailed towards Bembridge in flat seas, sandwich in one hand, wheel in the other. The sun shone, a teenage playlist blared out from the cockpit speakers and we made good progress. We took short turns on the helm to get used to the feel of

The chartered Beneteau Oceanis 37 handled beautifully
Rowan Hogbin

50 Rites of Passage

her; we last crossed in our UFO 34 – a very different vessel.

As we headed towards St Catherine's Point, the wind freshened and backed slightly. We shortened sail in anticipation and poked our nose out from the lee of the island. Even though we were clear of the overfalls south of the point, we were surprised by how quickly the seas built into a short chop. 'Always lumpier than you remember,' I mused. We donned extra fleeces and waterproofs, braced ourselves into comfortable spots and sat quietly, watching the Isle of Wight recede. Our youngest wound his arm round a secondary winch, curled up and disappeared inside his hood. No-one went below.

Soon we could make out a line of vessels in the nearest shipping lane ahead, travelling east to west. We freed off slightly to sail at right angles to the passing traffic. It is such a strange thing, crossing the shipping lanes; like a pedestrian walking across a busy motorway in slow motion.

The AIS on the cockpit chart plotter became the new screen time. 'Hey look, it's a tanker, 250m long, heading 256° at 12·2 knots, 5 miles and closing.' 'It's not going to hit us though' piped up the middle son. I was glad of that.

We remained vigilant as the light seeped out of the sky and we approached no-man's land between the lanes. We snacked on digestives, bananas and bottles of water.

The wind had dropped a bit, but with none of the promised north in it. Slowly, a procession of 'two whites and a red' appeared to our right. We continued across this second lane and watched our bearing to Alderney increase from 220° to 247°. We could only make a hopeless course of 147° in the strong, easterly spring tide. Our speed over the ground dropped to 3 knots and our weariness increased as we short tacked to little advantage. But spirits lifted as we saw the loom, then light of Cap de la Hague, visible 20 miles away from the French coast. A golden string of shore lights twinkled invitingly towards Cherbourg, but we were not tempted this time. Eventually, in the early hours, the tide turned in our favour. The southwesterly wind had dropped to Force 3 and, before we knew it, we were shooting west past Cap de La Hague at a ferocious rate, our speed over the ground (SOG) touching 9·6 knots at times.

Now 0430 and wide awake, we realised that unless we took action, we would arrive too early, mid-tide and in the dark, in danger of overshooting Braye and careering down The Swinge with its mess of overfalls and hazards.

We turned downwind to face the tide and the apparent wind dwindled to useless. Only one thing for it – we put the engine on and watched our SOG reduce dramatically along with our heart rates.

Alderney now lay astern of us, but we were tracking towards Braye steadily on the prescribed bearing of 215°. As light dawned and the current

The shipping lanes demand vigilance
Jane Russell

The Quénard Point light
Ros Hogbin

6 ACROSS THE ENGLISH CHANNEL

Arrival at Braye Harbour

Standard Port St Helier

HWS	+0040	HWN	+0050
LWS	+0025	LWN	+0105
MHWS	MHWN	MLWN	MLWS
–4·8m	–3·4m	–1·5m	–0·5m

Cap de la Hague, at the NW tip of the Cherbourg Peninsula, or its Gros du Raz light (Fl.5s48m23M Horn30s) will become visible well before you spot Alderney, which is low lying and slim from the NE. In the last few hours keep monitoring your ETA and factor in the combination of wind and tide to avoid being swept westwards into The Swinge and its dangerous overfalls or east into the top of The Race. By night, keep Casquets (Fl(5)30s37m18M) bearing no more than 260°T and Quénard Point light (Fl(4)15s12M) bearing no less than 120°T. Stay at least 0·5M offshore until you have identified Braye breakwater and the leading light/marks (front Q.8m9M, rear Q.17m12M; dayglo triangles) are aligned on 215°T.

Be vigilant for cross-set and stick closely to the transit to avoid the submerged remains of the breakwater extension.

Braye Harbour is sheltered in all but strong N-NE winds and swell. There are 70+ visitors' moorings and anchorage clear of the fairway. In season a water taxi operates 0800– 2359, call Mainbrayce VHF 37.

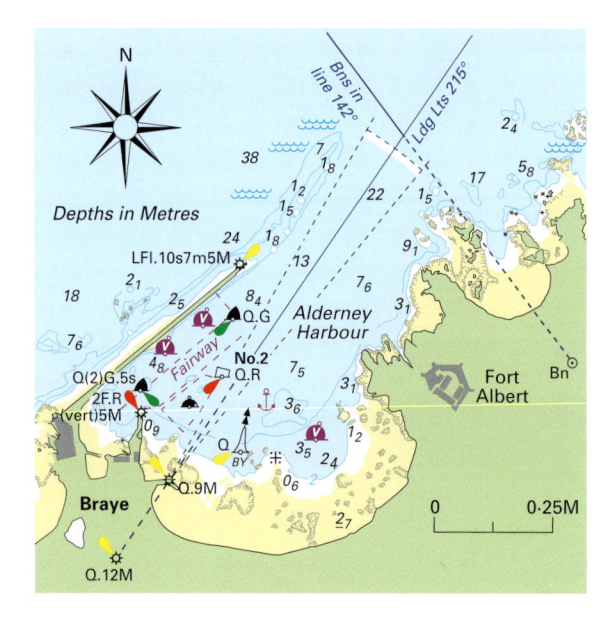

abated, we swung back round and lined up the leading lights, with the Quénard lighthouse flashing to port. Our eldest took the helm and guided us in. Our youngest remained oblivious, still clutching the winch.

By 0600, with the breakwater visible to starboard, we made our way into the safe embrace of Braye Harbour. We hooked a mooring buoy in the far corner and retreated below for hot chocolate and sleep. No cries of 'Beach, beach!' this time, just gentle snores and contentment.

The safe embrace of Braye Harbour, from Fort Albert
Ros Hogbin

52 Rites of Passage

The picture-perfect curve of white sand at Saye Bay
Ros Hogbin

WHY VISIT ALDERNEY?

In purely practical terms it's the nearest Channel Island to the south coast and the closest to France, so it makes sense to pull in to Braye Harbour first. Snug on your sturdy mooring or tucked away at anchor, you'll be ready to explore. Part of Alderney's charm is its friendliness and informality. Its size is key too. At three and a half miles long and one and a half miles wide, Alderney is perfectly proportioned - nowhere is too far away to visit.

Its beaches are legendary. Even Braye beach, a short walk from the harbour landing point, boasts soft, pale sand. The water is clear and calm in the lee of the long breakwater and there's enough in the way of facilities to keep families of all ages going 'til sundown. A walk, or short bike ride away you'll find many other beach options, such as Saye Bay near the campsite - picture-perfect curved white sand and enclosed by rocky headlands. Longy Bay is popular for kayaking and beach games at low tide and Corblets is an ace spot for rock pooling. All are underpopulated and super clean.

It's very easy to spend long days outside, exploring the island in the summer sun. There are plenty of shorter walks, or you can follow the beautiful ten mile coastal path that meanders down to beach level and up again to some incredible island-top views. Look out over the Alderney Race to France on one side and over the turbulent waters of the Swinge on the other. You may even spot the occasional sailing boat moving backwards, having mis-judged a foul tide!

Bike hire is easy and suitable for the whole family, giving you the freedom to discover more of the island's nooks and crannies in your own time. Or you can tour with a knowledgeable local guide.

Because of its strategic position, the island has a rich history – from a 4000 BC burial site and a well-preserved Roman small fort, to extensive Victorian and WWII forts and bunkers.

There's a working railway run by volunteers, which is an enjoyable way to visit the northeastern end of the island and the lighthouse at Quénard Point.

Up the hill from Braye lies the quaint and bustling village of St Anne, with cobbled street shopping and a small cinema offering regular evening viewings. Visit the Alderney Wildlife Trust on the main street and find out about the diverse range of plants and animals that thrive in the island's microclimate.

Alderney packs in a wide array of seasonal events, including Alderney Week at the beginning of August, with lots of activities for children, live music, parties and a carnival atmosphere. There are festivals to suit all tastes: literary, food and drink, wildlife and music. Eating and drinking span everything from the hearty Braye Chippy to gourmet à la carte, with cafés and bistros in between. There are pubs aplenty and ice cream vans beachside.

Down at the harbour, Alderney Sailing Club will become a regular haunt, welcoming you into their comfortable clubhouse for summer afternoon tea, or outside on their sail deck for a leisurely pint as the sun sets. And in the fullness of time, as the evening breeze ruffles your hair and you contemplate the day just passed, thoughts of moving on quietly recede into the distance.

www.visitalderney.com

6 ACROSS THE ENGLISH CHANNEL

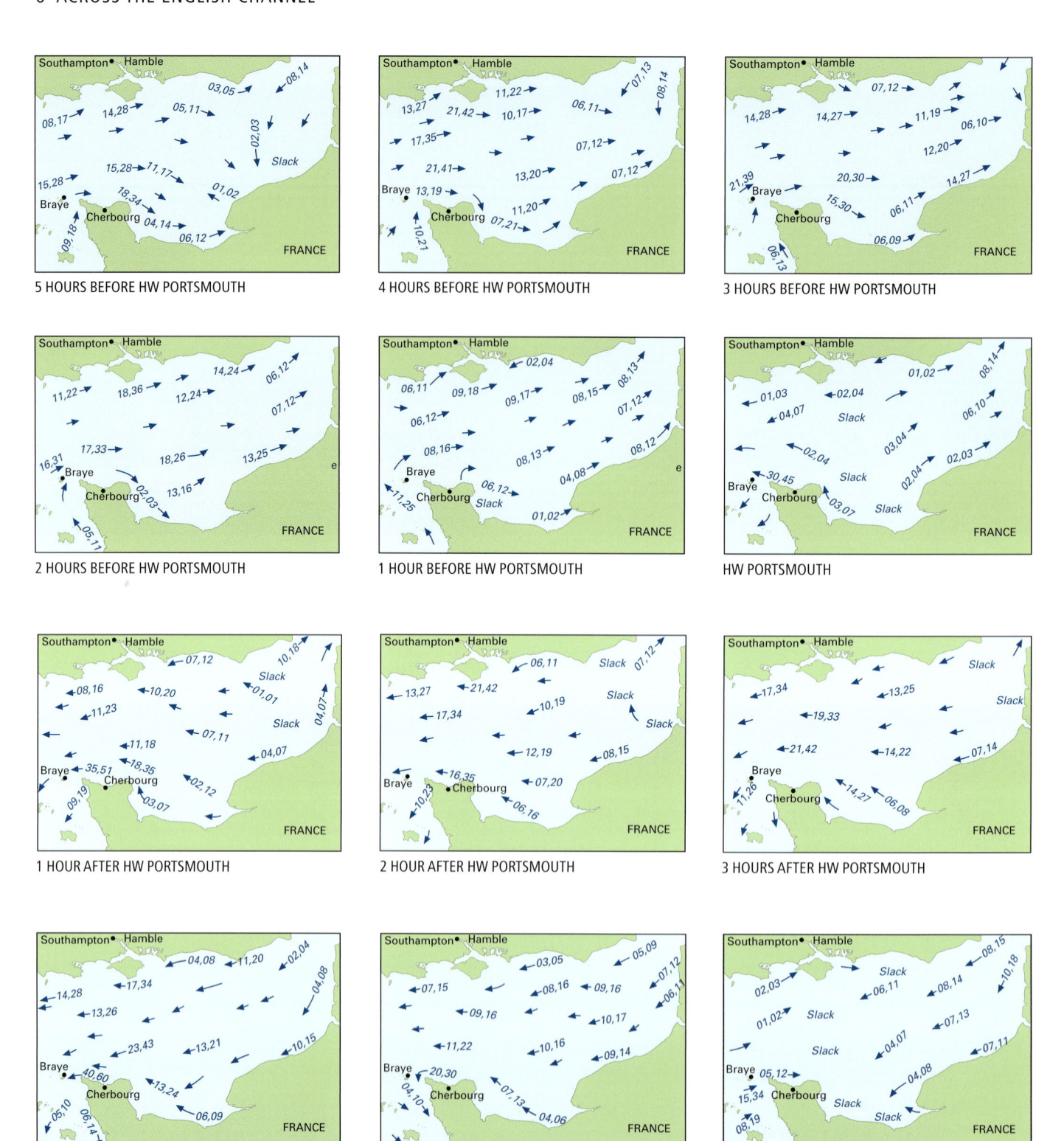

5 HOURS BEFORE HW PORTSMOUTH

4 HOURS BEFORE HW PORTSMOUTH

3 HOURS BEFORE HW PORTSMOUTH

2 HOURS BEFORE HW PORTSMOUTH

1 HOUR BEFORE HW PORTSMOUTH

HW PORTSMOUTH

1 HOUR AFTER HW PORTSMOUTH

2 HOUR AFTER HW PORTSMOUTH

3 HOURS AFTER HW PORTSMOUTH

4 HOURS AFTER HW PORTSMOUTH

5 HOURS AFTER HW PORTSMOUTH

6 HOURS AFTER HW PORTSMOUTH

TIDAL STREAMS

The figures shown against the arrows are the mean rates at neaps and springs in tenths of a knot. Thus 07,15 - mean neaps rate 0·7 knots, mean springs rate 1·5 knots

IMRAY TIDES PLANNER

Imray Tides Planner app is a useful planning tool. Download from the App Store or Google Play.

54 Rites of Passage

The inner moorings in Braye Harbour, with Braye beach beyond
Ros Hogbin

About the author

ROS HOGBIN first sailed across the Channel as a child, and continued to visit the Channel Islands through student days and beyond. Since then, her sailing has alternated between far flung and local. She completed a three year circumnavigation with her husband Andrew on their Nicholson 43, via the Pacific and Red Sea. She then returned to local waters to continue the cross-Channel tradition with their small boys in their UFO 34. Ros sailed with her family across the Mediterranean from Gibraltar to Turkey and spent subsequent holidays exploring the Turkish coast. She's currently enjoying revisiting Channel Island haunts with her teenagers.

Imray books and charts

Channel Islands, Cherbourg Peninsula and North Brittany
Peter Carnegie / Royal Cruising Club Pilotage Foundation (Imray)

These coasts can seem a daunting sailing area for those unaccustomed to their ways, but 'Carnegie's book provides reassurance and so much practical advice that anyone using it will feel confident of success.'

The Shell Channel Pilot
Tom Cunliffe (Imray)

'*Shell*' is more than a harbour guide. It also provides a reassuring hand on the shoulder for Channel navigation, with useful passage notes gleaned from the compiler's personal experience of more than 40 years running the tides and finding the eddies.

Chart packs (paper and digital)
2200 The Solent
2500 The Channel Islands and adjacent coast of France

Passage charts
C10	Western English Channel passage chart	1:400,000
C12	Eastern English Channel passage chart	1:300,000
C33A	Channel Islands	1:120,000

Imray Digital
ID20 English Channel

Across the North Sea

Garth Cooper

For the first-timer, a crossing of the North Sea to Holland, Belgium or Northern France from an east coast port can seem a daunting prospect. But with a bit of careful planning it can be a rewarding passage. It is certainly far from boring; in addition to all the usual navigation concerns, with coastal sand banks and narrow channels to be negotiated, it's also a pretty crowded piece of water, with wind farms sprouting up all over the place, and oil and gas rigs lit up at night like Christmas trees or looking like monsters out of *War of the Worlds* by day. Then there's the shipping lane; you may go for a couple of hours and not see a ship then suddenly, over the horizon, comes a gaggle of them, rather like London buses.

If you want to dip your toe into these waters, a trip from, say, Harwich to Oostende is a sensible summer's day sail of around 16 hours. A slightly longer passage is Harwich to IJmuiden from where, if you keep on going up the Noordzeekanaal, you can be in Amsterdam within 24 hours of leaving home. This is one of my regular routes, but it is different each time and, as ever, this passage can hold a few surprises.

I was helping to deliver a Jeanneau 37 for a friend. We chose to leave Woolverstone mid-afternoon to be at Landguard northerly cardinal at about high water to take advantage of the north-going ebb up to North Shipwash. The aim was to enter IJmuiden the following morning. The weather was looking kind, the wind in our favour from the southwest, about F4, and the sea a reasonably gentle and benign creature, which it often isn't; when the wind disagrees with the tide this can be an uncomfortable patch of water.

We had a very gentle run northeastwards in the flat water of the Sledway Channel, the tide helping us all the way as we passed east of the Cutler. Gybing at the Bawdsey buoy brought the early evening sunshine onto our stern and we adjusted our course to pass just north of North Shipwash and onto 076°T to head direct towards IJmuiden.

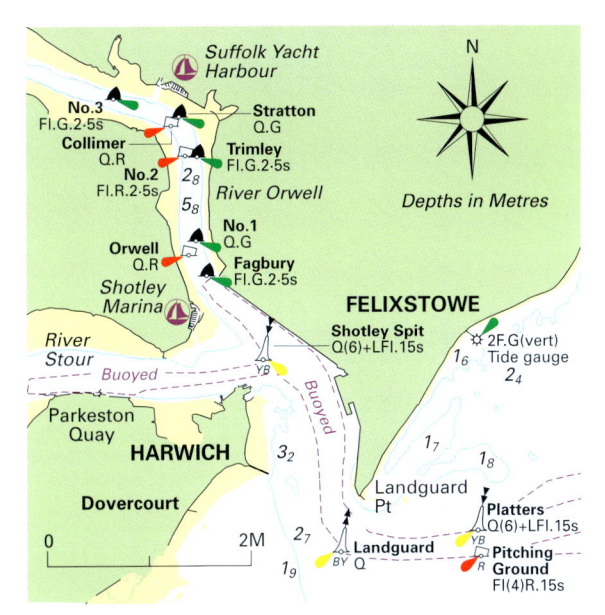

The thing to remember when crossing the North Sea is that tides ebb north and east and flood south and west. So, from here we were being pushed north of our rhumb line for about three hours or so before the tide changed to the south-going flood.

Nightfall can be an anxious time on any passage, but particularly if it's the first. This particular night was a stunner; we had clear skies and incredible visibility. With the change in the tide, the sun dropped behind us and I saw something I'd only ever seen in the Caribbean, the green flash.

I thought things couldn't get more memorable, but a couple of hours later an almost blood red moon popped up ahead of us. The light it shed was incredible and, to add to the pleasure of the moment, we realised that rising with the moon was the giant red planet itself, Mars. This was another first for me.

Such a clear light eases the anxiety of crossing the shipping lanes, which we were now into. I've had enough murky crossings, relying on AIS and radar, with the full crew alert on lookout duty, to be thankful of this jewel of a night. And if that

Opposite
Typical Netherlands cruising scene at Hindeloopen
Hilary Keatinge

Left
Looking NE across Felixstowe docks and Landguard Point, the departure point from Harwich out into the North Sea
Garth Cooper

7 ACROSS THE NORTH SEA

PASSAGE PLANNER
Departure from Harwich

Standard Port Walton

HWS	+0005	HWN	+0003
LWS	−0020	LWN	−0005

MHWS	MHWN	MLWN	MLWS
+0·2m	0·0m	−0·1m	−0·1m

Yachts leaving Harwich should use the recommended yacht channels and keep clear of commercial shipping. Maintain a listening watch on VHF 71 for *Harwich VTS*.

For a relatively comfortable North Sea crossing, wait for a period of settled southwesterlies. It is about 124M from Landguard buoy (Q) at the entrance to Harwich to the IJmuiden breakwaters. Tides in the North Sea run more or less NE on the ebb and SW on flood. Leave on the ebb and aim for a N-S-N-S sequence of three tidal changes to make the best use of the tidal sets. Slower boats will encounter a fourth change. Seas will build when wind is against tide and will quickly become uncomfortable as the wind strengthens, particularly at Springs. The Sledway Channel runs inshore of the Bawdsey Bank and is quieter than the main Shipway channel. From either NE Bawdsey (F.IG.10s) or at North Shipwash (Q Whis Racon (M) AIS), head onto 076°T. About 30M ENE of Shipwash you will pass through the southern end of the Anglia ONE windfarm before crossing the junction of the Deep Water Route (DWR) shipping lanes; to do so at the prescribed right angles will mean a slight adjustment to the course. The next significant mark is the NHR-N (RW) buoy (LFl.8s) which marks the NE edge of the North Hinder North TSS. Having sighted it, avoid it! At this point the tide should be pushing you well to the N of the TSS anyway. Monitor tidal set through the Rijnveld gas field and keep well clear of rigs and rig support boats.

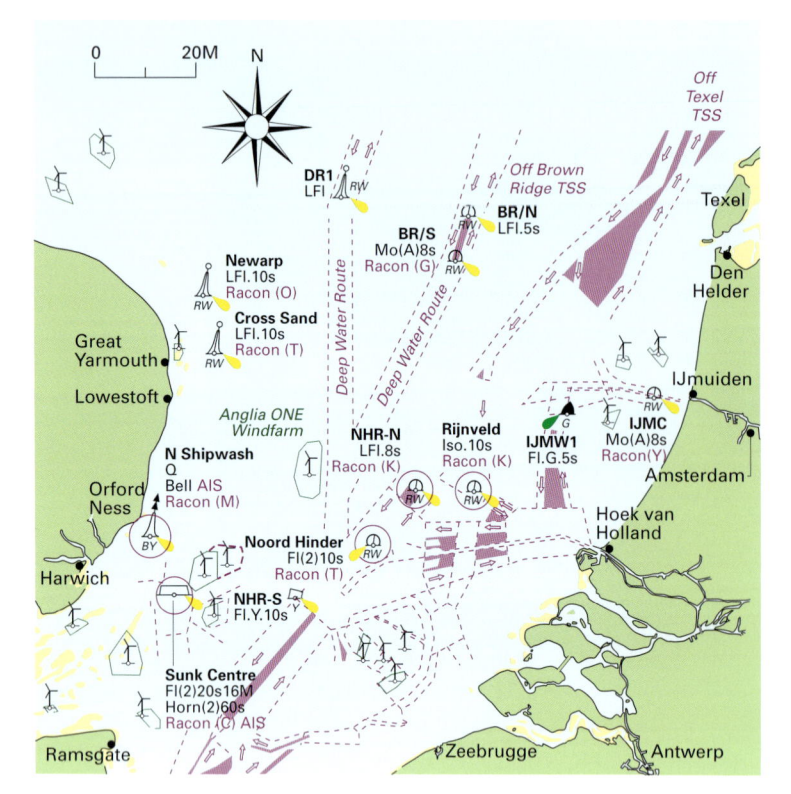

wasn't enough, we later watched the International Space Station rise in the southwest and, less than 10 minutes later, drop below the northeast horizon. Needless to say, we waved! Shining like a distant star it streaked across between us and the moon and Mars in total and eerie silence.

The flood brought with it a rather lumpy sea as the rising tide ran against the wind, but the next tidal change calmed the motion somewhat and set us north just nicely as we approached the top corner of the North Hinder North Traffic Separation Scheme (TSS). We had one moment of tension when a coaster came up behind us from the west and to all intents and purposes looked as if it was intent on ramming us. So, there was a joint sigh of relief when, about 250m away, it started to swing into the shipping channel and head away northeastwards, showing us a clean pair of heels.

East Anglia One under construction, typical of windfarm activity in the North Sea
Garth Cooper

58   Rites of Passage

North Sea gas rigs look like something out of *War of the Worlds*
Garth Cooper

Passing through the Rijn gas field and skirting the well-lit production platforms proved interesting, with the tide tending to push us down on a couple of the rigs. But with the light of the new day it became pretty relaxed sailing and a heated discussion began among the crew, two of whom were first timers across the North Sea, about when dawn actually occurred.

I maintain that the proper dawn occurs when the top edge of the sun rises above the horizon and that up to half an hour before this is the 'false' dawn. My two crew members, both retired scientific types, argued that as soon as they could see the deck and fittings it was daylight and dawn had thus occurred.

A rather late breakfast saw us past the IMJW1 buoy off the southeastern end of the IJmuiden crossing, which also marks the start of the Outer IJmuiden TSS. By coffee time we could see the low-lying outline of Holland, and more importantly the ships anchored north of the entry channel into IJmuiden awaiting instructions.

The tide was once more setting us south, so, sticking to the Dutch rules, we altered course slightly to clear north of the Luchterduinen windfarm. We headed in towards the chimneys of the cement factory and steelworks which lie to the north of the harbour entrance, passing just north of the large light tower (Fl.Y.5s), which lies about half a mile west of the entrance proper.

Approaching IJmuiden entrance
Garth Cooper

7 ACROSS THE NORTH SEA

Arrival at IJmuiden

Standard Port Vlissingen
HW +0102   HWN +0232

MHWS	MHWN	MLWN	MLWS
–2·7m	–2·3m	–0·7m	–0·2m

At the green IJMW1 buoy (Fl.G5s) adjust course to stay south of the Outer and Inner IJ - Guel entrance channel TSS and north of the Luchterduinen windfarm. Unlike in UK waters, passing through windfarms is strictly forbidden here. A safe water buoy IJMC (RW) Mo(A)8s, Racon(Y) lies about 5M west of the harbour, but a more useful final waypoint is about 50 metres N of the large yellow beacon tower (Fl.Y.5s) which lies 0·5M west of the southern breakwater into IJmuiden.

IJmuiden is a major commercial port, with ferry and container vessel traffic. It's main appeal is that it is an entry point for the Noordzeekanaal and thereby all the interconnected inland waterways of the Netherlands.

Berthing is available at Seaport Marina which lies inside the inner breakwater. Alternatively, continue on to the Zuidersluis lock (VHF 22) to enter the Noordzeekanaal and continue 15M to Amsterdam.

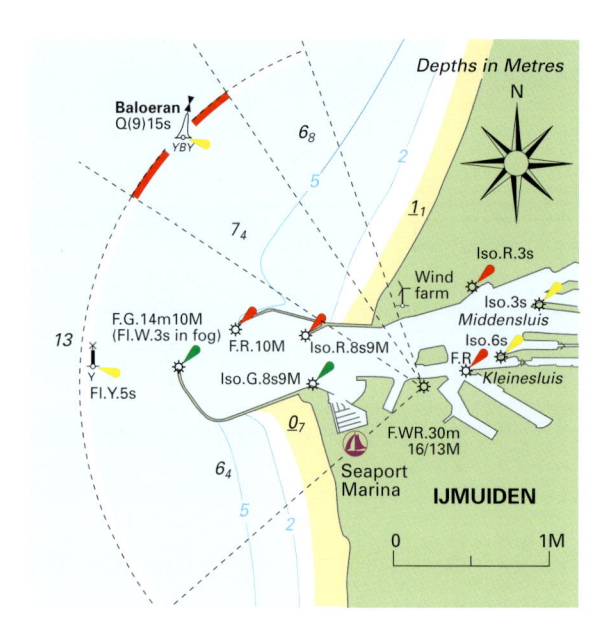

We had arrived. But the day was still young, so we passed straight through the harbour catching the Zuiderhuis lock into the Noordzeekanaal. By mid-afternoon we were sipping beers in our favourite stopping place, the 'new' Amsterdam Marina on the north bank of the river, only a short ferry ride to the heart of the city. From casting off to tying up was just short of 24 hours.

WHY VISIT THE NETHERLANDS?

Why do I go across the often cold, grey North Sea to the Netherlands, when I've got the best coastal sailing in England on my doorstep? First off: variety. Second: the desire to explore and meet new people. Third: to enjoy a different culture - and the food's good too.

I travel to the Netherlands at least once or twice a year. Apart from the very odd occasion, the trips across have been enjoyable and interesting, if something of a challenge at times. The Dutch are particularly welcoming and usually make our passage into the country as easy and smooth as possible.

Amsterdam never sleeps. Taking part in the Night Convoy, the only time that yachts with masts can transit the city north or south in the middle of the night as bridges open in sequence, is an experience not to miss. Of course, if you

Entering Nordzeekanaal through Kleine Sluis
Garth Cooper

have a motor cruiser, or can easily drop your mast, then the extensive canal system open to you is vast; you can transit the Netherlands to Germany, Belgium and down into France.

We have nothing in the UK to compare to the inland waterways of the Netherlands. The Norfolk Broads are a mere shadow of what the Dutch have to play with. For many, sailing on the shallow inland seas, the Markermeer and the IJsselmeer, with average depths of only four or five metres, is a new experience. Something to be aware of is that, because they are so shallow, when it does blow up the seas become steep and short and extremely uncomfortable. But all through the waterways there are attractive and delightful towns to visit. Urk on the east coast of the IJsselmeer was once an island and still likes to call itself so. It has an extremely good fish restaurant that we always make a bee-line for. Another favourite is Stavoren where the town dock and quay is the place to moor. There is a large marina but it's on the other side of town.

Places such as Hoorn, Enkhuizen, with its outdoor rural museum; Edam, famous for its cheese and with a welcoming yacht club marina; Makuum which likes to think of itself as still an island where the locals dress in traditional costumes on special days; Lelystad, which, like Enkhuizen, is a gateway into the IJsselmeer from the Markermeer via huge ship locks, and is where a series of museums tell the stories of the building of the polders and the country's maritime history, not to mention the Aviodrome aerospace museum.

IJmuiden is really a gateway to another world, to a place where you can sail in relatively protected and non-tidal waters, and with a multitude of places to stop to explore.

Hindeloopen
Hilary Keatinge

Classics race on the IJsselmeer
Hilary Keatinge

7 ACROSS THE NORTH SEA

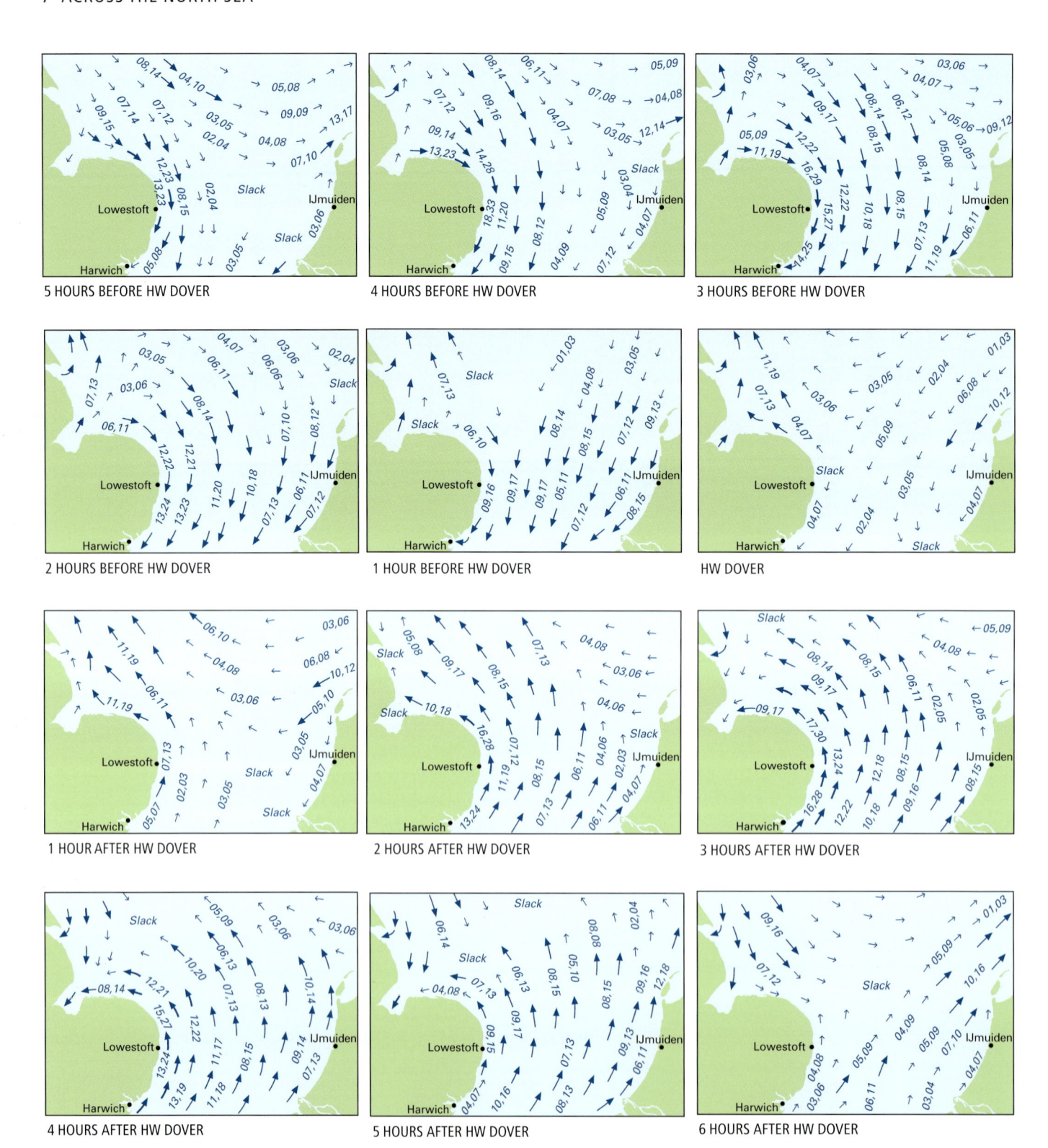

5 HOURS BEFORE HW DOVER

4 HOURS BEFORE HW DOVER

3 HOURS BEFORE HW DOVER

2 HOURS BEFORE HW DOVER

1 HOUR BEFORE HW DOVER

HW DOVER

1 HOUR AFTER HW DOVER

2 HOURS AFTER HW DOVER

3 HOURS AFTER HW DOVER

4 HOURS AFTER HW DOVER

5 HOURS AFTER HW DOVER

6 HOURS AFTER HW DOVER

TIDAL STREAMS

The figures shown against the arrows are the mean rates at neaps and springs in tenths of a knot. Thus 07,15 - mean neaps rate 0·7 knots, mean springs rate 1·5 knots

IMRAY TIDES PLANNER

Imray Tides Planner app is a useful planning tool. Download from the App Store or Google Play.

62 Rites of Passage

HARWICH TO IJMUIDEN

Waiting for the green light before the Den Oever lock, one of two transits between The IJsselmeer and the tidal Waddenzee
Hilary Keatinge

About the author

GARTH COOPER is a writer and broadcaster who has sailed his entire life. He trained as a boatbuilder, went on to be a senior agricultural journalist, a BBC broadcaster, editorial director of a publishing company then, in a shift in career, wrote for sailing magazines before becoming editor of Anglia Afloat. He sails a Contest 33. He is co-author of the *East Coast Pilot* and the new author of *North Sea Passage Pilot*. He is a skipper with the East Anglian Sailing Trust, taking blind people sailing. When not writing or sailing he helps run the family farm in Norfolk. He is a member of the Yachting Journalists' Association, RYA and the Cruising Association.

Imray books and charts

East Coast Pilot
Garth Cooper and Dick Holness (Imray)

Not only does it cover the many harbours, rivers and creeks, it also reveals some of the mysteries of sailing these shallow and shifting coastal waters, with unique 'rolling road' diagrams to guide the approach showing buoyage sequences and tracks to steer into rivers and ports.

Cruising Guide to the Netherlands
Brian Navin (Imray)

Regarded as the authoritative companion for anyone cruising the Netherlands using fixed mast routes. This guide is based on popular selected routes which offer an opportunity to visit most of the regions of the Netherlands from the estuary of the Schelde up to the IJsselmeer and Waddensee.

Inland Waterways of the Netherlands
Louise Busby & David Broad (Imray)

The Netherlands offers one of the most extensive yet compact cruising grounds in Europe. This book is a user's guide to the whole network excluding only those waterways which offer less than 3·5m bridge height. www.inlandwaterwaysofthenetherlands.com is kept up to date with details of changes to the waterways along with useful links to further information.

Chart packs (paper and digital)
2000 Suffolk and Essex
2120 North Sea – Nieuwpoort to Den Helder

Passage chart
C25 Harwich to River Humber and Holland   1:340,000

Imray Digital
ID10 North Sea

Rites of Passage 63

Across the western English Channel

Jason Lawrence

FALMOUTH TO L'ABER WRAC'H

Thoughts of new lands beyond the distant horizon are pretty appealing. It's one thing to mosey down the south coast experiencing slight variations of a familiar theme, quite another to make landfall in a completely different country. Such a passage always feels rewarding, with the expectation of new adventure and cultural delectation beyond.

My destination was L'Aber Wrac'h, 90-odd miles from Falmouth, the gateway to the Chenal du Four. At a speed of 6 knots it looked likely to take around 15 hours. Having looked at the charts and read the pilot the entrance looked tricky with leading lines, marks to make, and narrow channels through a mass of rocks, with disaster waiting on the slightest mistake. Sitting in Falmouth it looked daunting. How much did I really want to go to L'Aber Wrac'h? On arrival I would definitely want the assistance of daylight, and with French time being BST +1 hour I would also want plenty of time to secure my S&S 35 *Slamat* safely alongside before securing myself a table in a nearby restaurant. So, assuming I hoped to arrive at 1600 BST, I would need to leave Falmouth by 0100. The tide would be flooding, and in the forecasted easterly winds I could expect wind against tide and a lumpy sea, but that was as it was. With the alarm set for midnight I set out for dinner ashore - fish and chips at the Harbour Lights.

I was on the northern wharf of Falmouth Haven Marina, and with many moored boats close by it would require a careful exit from the berth. Luckily the wind was light in the protection of the harbour. After making coffee I slowly sprung the bows off and tiptoed through the moorings to the clearer water of the channel out to Carrick Roads. Motoring gently, I raised the main with one reef in. With a good Force 4 I had no need to be overburdened.

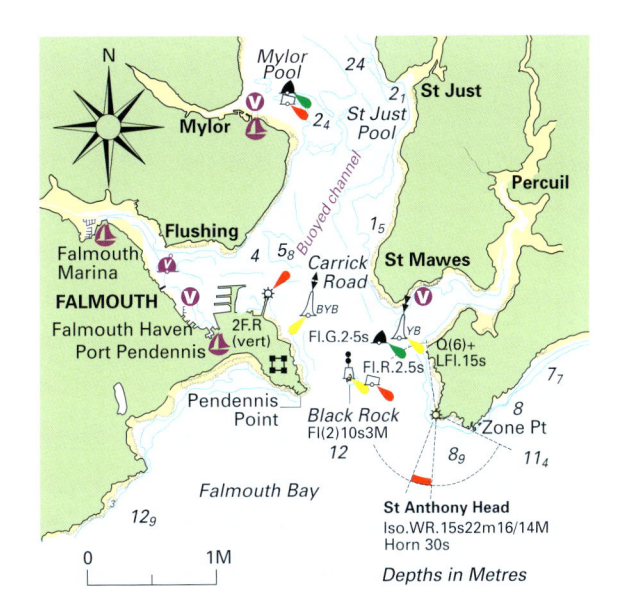

I had noted a number of fishing buoys in the western entrance, so I chose to sail down the main channel and out past St Anthony Head to ensure no early calamity. Once we were into the wind and swell *Slamat* was quite lively, so I shortened the headsail to ease the motion and settled down to navigate past various obstructions; a charted tidal power obstruction and some anchored shipping.

By 0130 we were clear ahead, out past the 50m contour, and the seas moderated to a

Opposite
Anchored under Fort de Latte, Cap Frehel
Shutterstock
Nyokki

Below
Falmouth Customs Quay with the Harbour Lights cafe far left
Jason Lawrence

Rites of Passage 65

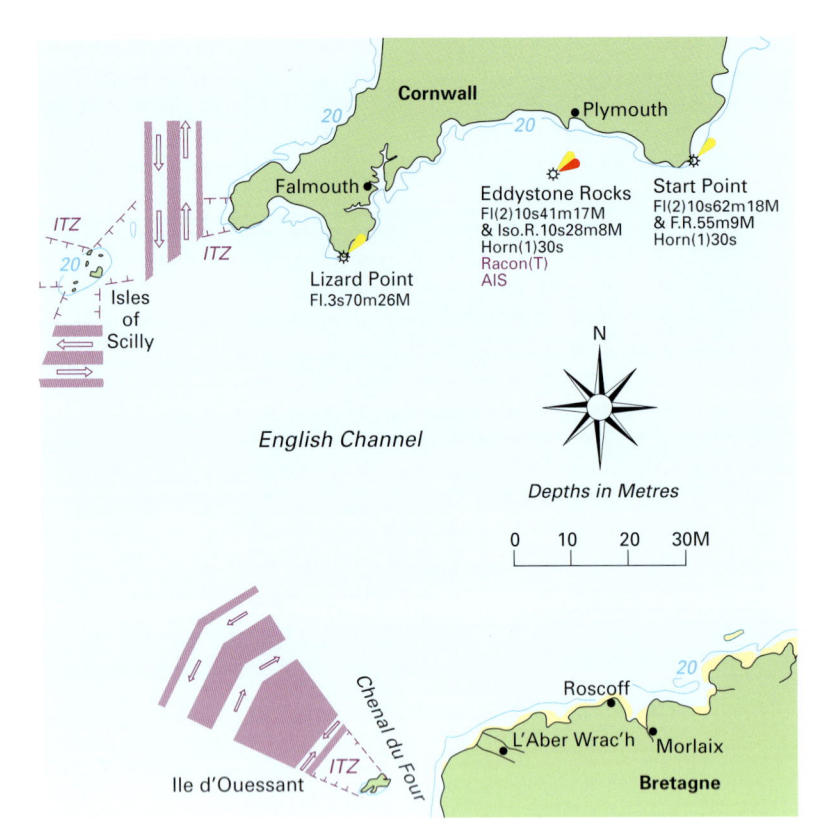

8 ACROSS THE WESTERN ENGLISH CHANNEL

PASSAGE PLANNER
Departure from Falmouth

Standard Port Plymouth

| HWS | −0043 | HWN | −0025 |
| LWS | −0009 | LWN | −0009 |

MHWS	MHWN	MLWN	MLWS
−0·4m	−0·3m	−0·4m	−0·3m

With a passage of this length it is more important than ever to be sure that you have a window of reasonable weather. Ideally wait for a period when winds have a northerly component and avoid fog if at all possible.

You'll have slightly uneven amounts of westerly and easterly tidal sets, depending on your timings. Study the tidal atlas and compensate for the stronger sets on the corner of Brittany. The Channel shipping lanes are also much busier on the French side from the top of the Ouessant Traffic Separation Scheme (TSS). In poor visibilty be aware that rocky shoals extend as far as 3M out from the French coast.

comfortable 1-1·5m with the wind from the east at 14 knots. We were close hauled, but making 175° and on course for L'Aber Wrac'h. With the Lizard Point light over my right shoulder we were free of the lee shore and I was happy with our progress, clocking over 6 knots. By 0500 we were crossing the west-going shipping, and there were plenty of working fishing boats to keep me busy. I was glad of the AIS to help make sense of them all.

Time for a coffee, then dawn! And with the wind backing I could crack off, reducing the heel and improving comfort. The wind vane was working well, so with a clear horizon I settled down for a short nap. By 0800 the wind had eased and backed further, so I shook out the reef and we pushed on, making over 7 knots and bettering our average.

Now over halfway, we were making very good progress. The sun had come out, the water a jade green, and with the wind on the beam we were having a great sail. We were starting to see some eastbound shipping, which we expected to see more of. There were little clusters of fishing boats but nothing too concerning, so it was time for some ship's lunch; bread, pâté, cheese, cold meats and pickles… lovely.

Early afternoon saw conditions change. The wind was increasing and with the tide setting to the east again the sea was getting up. It was now blowing Force 5 and quite lumpy. I put in a reef and approached the coast with caution. The French coast is littered with rocks but the dangers are well marked, it's just a case of finding the right beacon. By 1400, with 20 odd miles to go, I could clearly see a large obelisk on the horizon. I

Grand Pot de Buerre port hand beacon
Nick Chavasse

66 Rites of Passage

Petit Pot de Buerre cardinal beacon with the obelisk on Petite Île beyond
Nick Chavasse

took this to be the light tower Île Vierge, and I knew that L'Aber Wrac'h entrance was about 3 miles to the west. The first mark I was looking for was the Libenter westerly cardinal mark. I found it and left it to port, giving the outlying rocks to the northeast a good berth. In the lee of the rocks, the seas quickly moderated. Despite my earlier anxieties, the entrance was actually quite straightforward. From Libenter it was just a question of following the Grand Chenal leading marks in on about 100°T to Plate port hand beacon, and then turning south-east down the broad, well-marked channel to the marina.

It was now blowing 25 knots, so I rounded up and dropped the main early. I planned on an inside berth on the visitors' pontoon, facing upriver and east-south-east into the wind. This would be port side to, but meant turning around in the restricted space inside the marina, good to know my Volvo engine kicks to starboard. With much throttle and tiller movement I managed to push the bows round into the wind and gently glide alongside and at 1700 BST I turned off the engine, very happy to be safely tucked up in L'Aber Wrac'h. We had covered 101 miles on the GPS over some 16·5 hours dock to dock.

Visitors' berths inside the wavebreaker pontoon in L'Aber Wrac'h marina and visitor mooring buoys in the river beyond
Jason Lawrence

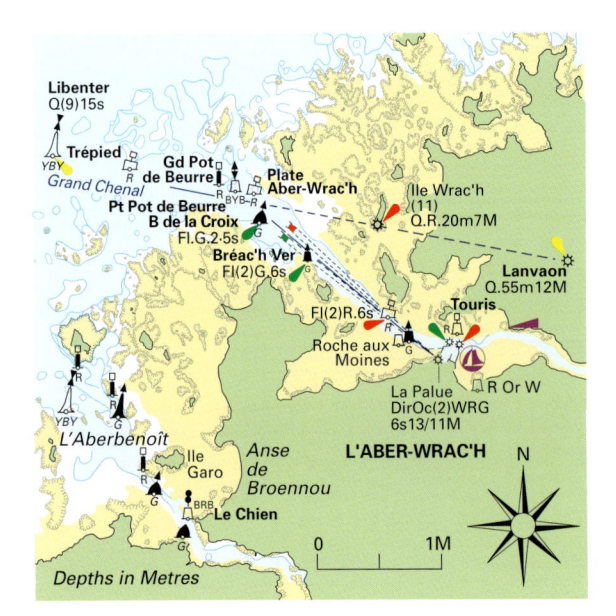

8 ACROSS THE WESTERN ENGLISH CHANNEL

Arrival at L'Aber Wrac'h

Standard Port Brest

HW	+0030	LW	+0038
MHWS	MHWN	MLWN	MLWS
+0.7m	+0.6m	+0.1m	–0.1m

L'Aber Wrac'h is accesible at all states of the tide via the Grand Chenal. Île Vierge (Fl.5s77m27M AIS), lies 3M NNE of the Libenter W card buoy (Q(9)15s) which marks the start of the channel. The entrance is wide, well-marked and has plenty of depth. In visibility of 5 miles or more the leading marks and lights are clearly visible and entry is straightforward, day or night. Make allowance for the accelerated tidal streams along this section of coast, which will tend to set you sideways across the approaches. From Libenter steer a course of 100°T on the leading line of Île Wrac'h (QR20m7M) with Lanvaon (QW55m12M) on the hill beyond. Leave Trépied and the two Pots de Buerre to port then pass between Plate Aber Wrac'h and the lit starboard buoy Basse de la Croix (Fl G 2.5s) to pick up the sector light leading in on 128°T.

There are visitor moorings for vessels up to 18m on the north (port) side of the channel opposite the marina. Anchoring is only allowed to the W of the lifeboat slip.

Harbour launch VHF 09

There is something elemental about West Brittany, with her rugged granite coastline and strong tides. Ashore, there is a distinct village feel, far removed from the beaten track, centred around sailing and the sea, good food and its production. I could now look forward to short day passages, interesting navigation, and remote anchorages, interspersed with town marinas where I would dust off my French and break out the euros.

It was time to freshen up and then head out for dinner: 'Une douzaine d'huîtres, salade de Chèvre et un petit café noir s'il vous plaît!'

Final approach to L'Aber Wrac'h
Jason Lawrence

68 Rites of Passage

L'Aber Wrac'h entrance, looking northwest
Nick Chavasse

WHY VISIT L'ABER WRAC'H?

Arriving in Brittany always carries an air of excitement and expectation, where experience and reward await. L'Aber Wrac'h is a great place to start. Whether heading south to Brest and beyond, or east towards the ancient city of St Malo, Brittany opens up like a good book.

As a child this family cruise was always a highlight of my summer. Strong memories of warm sunny days and white sandy beaches, historic towns with different traditions, new tastes and unfamiliar language. For my father it brought plenty of sailing with short day passages and quiet anchorages. For my mother, stunning scenery, culture, food and music. Today our roles have changed but Brittany remains a rewarding and satisfying destination for the whole family.

The towns have a medieval feel where history runs deep. From the many anchorages and marinas there are opportunities to explore inland by foot or bus, and one is never too far from a friendly cafe or restaurant. Relatively remote as a region, Brittany is comparatively less populated than English cruising destinations, so solitude can also be found, and with fewer cruisers it is still possible to find a quiet anchorage upriver to enjoy a moment of peace as the sun sets on another day.

Brittany has strong agricultural traditions with most towns having market day selling fresh local produce, dairy being particularly good. Coastal towns offer oyster, lobster and crevette. Many happy cockpit meals have been enjoyed with this simple fare, perhaps with a bottle of local wine.

It is easy to flow from the solitude of the anchorage one day, to the bustle of a local fête the next. From historic maritime festivals to simple rural gatherings, fêtes are a feature of the Breton summer and it is not uncommon to join large communal tables to eat and drink cider with the locals and then dance the Breton dance.

The stunning scenery changes as you move along the coast. Whether it's the beach at Carantec, the Rade de Morlaix with its intricate navigation, or a journey upriver to the ancient city of Morlaix itself, there are plenty of options for all tastes. One of my favourites is the Côtes-d'Armor, with the beautiful and scenic Ploumanac'h at its heart. Huge pink granite boulders set a dramatic entrance, and with the right tide and a shallow draft, a safe haven and interesting town awaits.

Continuing eastwards, open water passages or river navigation offer countless options while slowly meandering on to the walled city of St Malo. Many books have been written of its history and local importance, but for us it ended our summer cruise and afforded an opportunity to stock up on French treats before a hop to the Channel Islands and a return to the Solent.

Truly, a summer cruise along the Brittany coast makes the Channel crossing to get there a definitive rite of passage.

8 ACROSS THE WESTERN ENGLISH CHANNEL

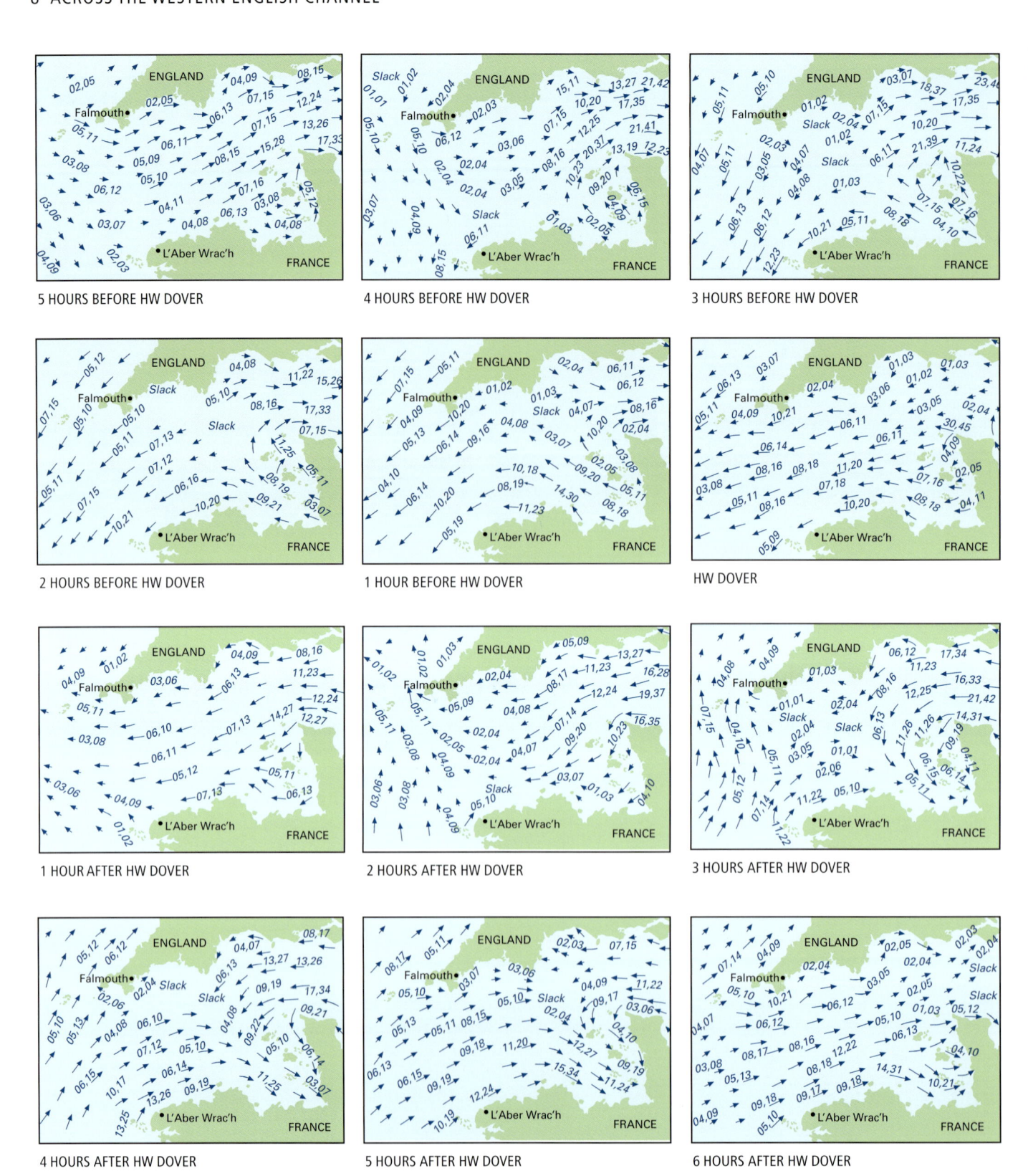

5 HOURS BEFORE HW DOVER

4 HOURS BEFORE HW DOVER

3 HOURS BEFORE HW DOVER

2 HOURS BEFORE HW DOVER

1 HOUR BEFORE HW DOVER

HW DOVER

1 HOUR AFTER HW DOVER

2 HOURS AFTER HW DOVER

3 HOURS AFTER HW DOVER

4 HOURS AFTER HW DOVER

5 HOURS AFTER HW DOVER

6 HOURS AFTER HW DOVER

TIDAL STREAMS

The figures shown against the arrows are the mean rates at neaps and springs in tenths of a knot. Thus 07,15 - mean neaps rate 0·7 knots, mean springs rate 1·5 knots

IMRAY TIDES PLANNER

Imray Tides Planner app is a useful planning tool. Download from the App Store or Google Play.

Rites of Passage

FALMOUTH TO L'ABER WRAC'H

Stunning scenery and a rich history. Old sailing boat in the bay of Roscoff from Île de Batz
*Shutterstock
J J Farq*

About the author

JASON LAWRENCE had an early fascination with the sea, kindled on the Isle of Wight and family holidays along the coast of Northern France. After crewing for others on transatlantic passages, in 2000 he completed a singlehanded transatlantic which set the scene for plans to sail around the world, and in 2007 circumstances allowed that ambition to take shape. With his wife and two young children they set off on their catamaran, returning to the UK in 2013. Family life and obligations on shore have restricted long distance sailing, but now with an S&S 35, Jason and family are once again exploring the wonderful cruising grounds on their doorstep.

Imray books and charts

Channel Islands, Cherbourg Peninsula and North Brittany
Peter Carnegie / Royal Cruising Club Pilotage Foundation (Imray)

These coasts can seem a daunting sailing area for those unaccustomed to their ways, but 'Carnegie's book provides reassurance and so much practical advice that anyone using it will feel confident of success.'

Atlantic France
Ouessant to the Spanish Border
Nick Chavasse / Royal Cruising Club Pilotage Foundation (Imray)

The authoritative cruising companion for this long and varied coastline with its sometimes-daunting tides and currents … welcomed both by first-time visitors to the region and by old hands who are revisiting their favourite haunts.

Chart packs (paper and digital)
2400 West Country
2500 The Channel Islands and adjacent coast of France
2510 North Brittany

Passage charts
C18 Western approaches to English Channel 1:1,000,000
C10 Western English Channel passage chart 1:400,000
C35 C35 Baie de Morlaix to L'Aber-Ildut 1:75,000

Imray Digital
ID20 The English Channel

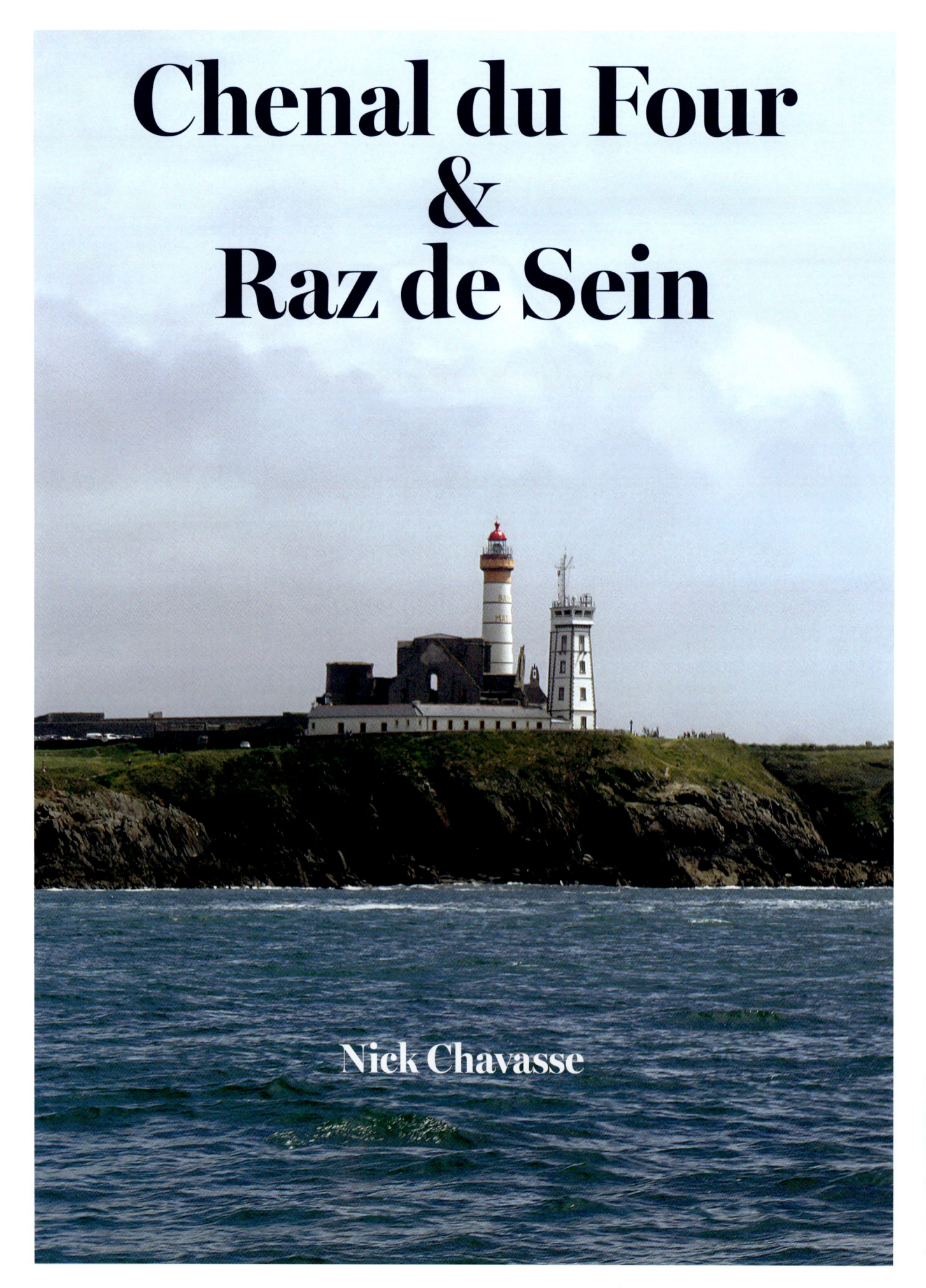

Chenal du Four & Raz de Sein

Nick Chavasse

L'ABERWRAC'H TO AUDIERNE

To the cruising sailor there is no greater sense of achievement, no less significant rite of passage, than a first passage through both the Chenal du Four and the Raz de Sein in one go.

The ideal conditions for this feat include a fresh breeze with a touch of north in it, good visibility and a favourable tide for as long as you can muster. A first look at all the charted hazards is enough to make you doubt the whole plan but rest assured that the channels are wide and deep, and navigation is not as difficult as it might first appear.

L'Aber Wrac'h is a popular departure point but we had been enjoying the solitude of Paludin, two miles up river on board our Bowman 40, *Wild Bird*. We slipped the mooring just after 0630 as the tide in the river began to turn and we headed downstream with the start of the ebb. The wind was mainly westerly and moderate but the skies were grey and muggy. The purist may not approve but, leaving L'Aber Wrac'h estuary and the Libenter buoy behind, some help from the iron topsail felt like a sensible pre-requisite until we were clear of the many reefs which crowd this corner. The tide was still just setting ENE but with wind and tide in harmony the sea was relatively calm and the swell was slight. Much to the consternation of my crew of many years of married life, I briefly considered the possibility of taking the Portsall Inner Passage, which leaves the Roches de Portsall, infamous for the *Amoco Cadiz* disaster, and Le Four lighthouse to starboard. But this is not advised for first-timers. The more conventional route outside the Roches de Portsall adds only a couple of miles and on reflection seemed sufficiently challenging given our wider goal.

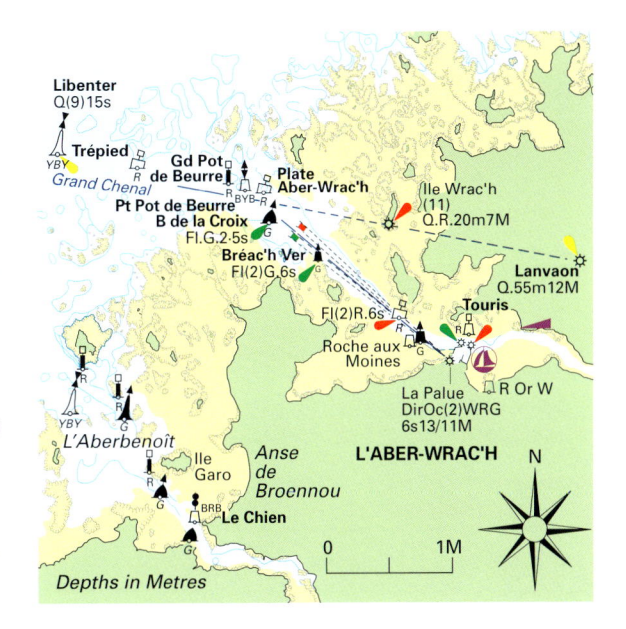

At first we made rather slow progress outside all of these dangers towards the westerly cardinal of Grande Basse Portsall but then the WSW ebb set began to help and we settled onto starboard and freed off a bit towards the brooding, grey tower of Le Four, aiming to leave it about half a mile to port. The Chenal du Four is flanked by the Iroise Islands of Île d'Ouessant, Île Molène and their smaller sisters and once we were south of Le Four their protection from even the slight groundswell began to be noticeable and the water flattened out. We had been advised to make a list of the buoys beforehand and tick them off as we passed; 'Follow the marked channel, watch for

Opposite
Pointe de St-Mathieu at the southern end of the Chenal du Four
Nick Chavasse

Below
Looking NW over the approaches to L'Aberwrac'h
Nick Chavasse

Rites of Passage 73

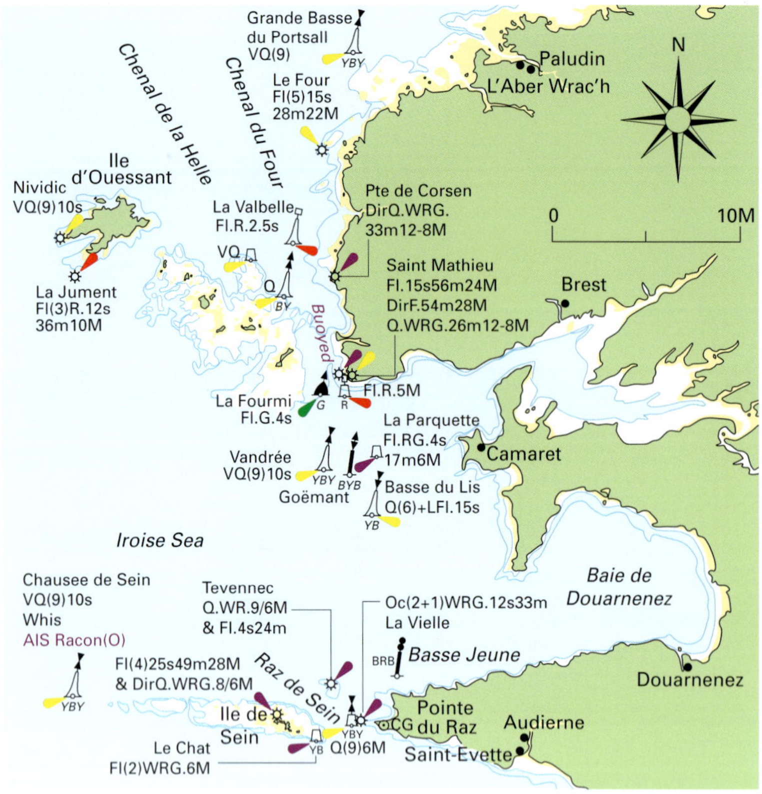

9 CHENAL DU FOUR AND RAZ DE SEIN

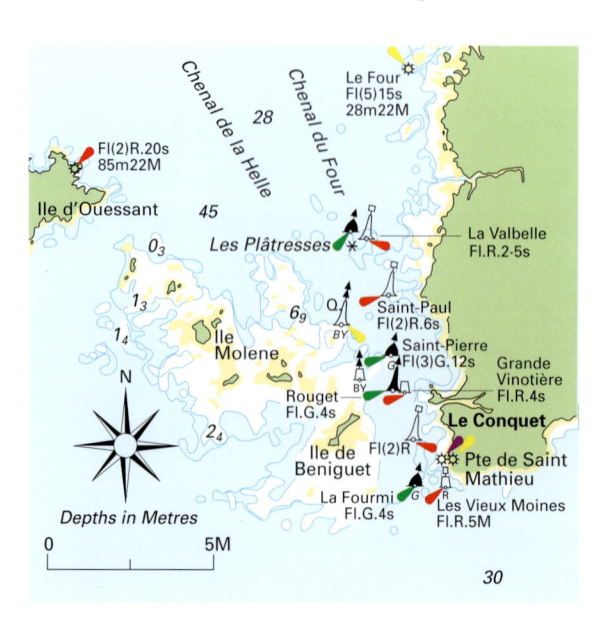

PASSAGE PLANNER

Departure from L'Aber Wrac'h

Standard Port Brest

HW	+0030	LW	+0038
MHWS	MHWN	MLWN	MLWS
+0·7m	+0·6m	+0·1m	–0·1m

Make allowance for the accelerated tidal streams along this section of coast, which will tend to set you sideways across the entrance.

The most exposed part of this passage is between L'Aber Wrac'h and Le Four. The whole area is prone to fog. Tides are key to timings.

Chenal du Four

The tide turns at St-Mathieu earlier than it does in the north of Le Four. Southbound this is a nuisance because the early part of the south stream runs to waste. Northbound the tidal lag is a benefit and extends the fair tide by a couple of hours.

Plan for a favourable tide for as much of the Four as timings allow, but if winds are on the nose aim to go through the narrow part between Le Conquet and St-Mathieu at slack because wind over tide here can create very steep seas, particularly at Springs when the stream can run at up to 5 knots. If you need to sit out the tide there are anchorages in Anse de Porsmoguer, Portz-Illien or Anse des Blancs Sablons.

On a first passage, in bad conditions or in poor visibility it is better to stick to the channel markers and leading lines, but be aware that in poor visibility the marks themselves become a hazard.

---

tidal drift, and then head south when Le Conquet is nearly on the beam to port.' Once we were onto the tidal conveyor belt we were glad to have done our homework: La Valbelle to port and we eased the sheets again to keep Les Plâtresses rocks well to starboard. We ticked off St Paul then St Pierre and in no time at all we were passing the massive red bulk of the Grande Vinotière tower.

The tide was now beginning to slacken but with the wind on the beam it was pleasant sailing southwards under the imposing gaze of Pointe de Saint-Mathieu with its two towers and ruined abbey buildings. The tide turns here much earlier than it does at the top of the Four, but we had made it, and once past La Fourmi starboard hand marker we found ourselves in the open Iroise sea.

Le Four Lighthouse stands sentinel at the northern end of the channel
Nick Chavasse

74 Rites of Passage

Raz de Sein

Tidal streams across the Iroise are generally weaker than in the Four or through the Raz. Aim to be at the Raz at slack water with the turn to your favour. If you arrive at the end of the tide you risk the gate closing against you. If this happens the safe options are Morgat or Douarnenez. In settled weather anchorages on Île de Sein or in Baie des Trépassés are also a possibility. The Raz can be rough even in moderate conditions, and in strong wind against tide the overfalls become dangerous. At neaps, with calms or light winds and with no swell it is less turbulent, but you would want to feel confident in your engine should it be needed.

The distance across the Iroise between the two tidal gates at Pointe de Saint-Mathieu and Raz de Sein is about 18 miles. We were aiming to be at the Raz an hour before high water Brest, when it would be relatively slack but beginning to turn in our favour. If we had any doubts, now was a moment to change our minds and turn eastwards into Camaret or Brest, but it wasn't yet lunchtime, the promised blue skies had finally arrived and we had all afternoon to play with.

As we crossed the main Brest approach channel the long, low ocean swell returned. For the next few hours the tide was against us and even though we still had wind on the beam our speed over ground dropped to less than 4 knots. But this suited our timings, so after lunch we took turns to snooze in the sun. A steady procession of boats was heading northwards – an easier direction to make the passage in one because of the tidal lag at the top of the Four which gives a few extra hours of tide.

A series of islets, rocks and shoals extend WSW from both Pointe de Toulinguet and Pointe de Penhir, but they are well marked. We passed through leaving Goemant to starboard. The monochrome lighthouse on Île de Sein appeared off our bow, but there was no sign of any island beneath it. In contrast the higher ground of Cap Sizun running down to the Pointe du Raz was increasingly domineering. Windswept and treeless it belied the cosy harbour of Douarnenez, which we knew was tucked in only 15 miles to leeward. There was a moment of doubt when we questioned our timings and thought about

Douarnenez offers a cosy retreat
Binna Graham

9 CHENAL DU FOUR AND RAZ DE SEIN

Arrival at Audierne

Standard Port Brest

HW	-0032	LW	-0032
MHWS	MHWN	MLWN	MLWS
–1·8m	–1·4m	–0·7m	–0·3m

The approach to Ste Evette and Audierne is relatively straightforward and well marked. Keep Kergadec (DirQ.WRG.43m12-19M) in line with the old lighthouse to lead you in clear of the end of the breakwater. In any swell, seas break on La Gamelle. There are visitor moorings and an anchorage at Ste Evette and a marina up river in the friendly town of Audierne. The channel to Audierne is partially lit but arrival after dark is not recommended for the first-timer; it would be better to anchor at Ste Evette overnight.

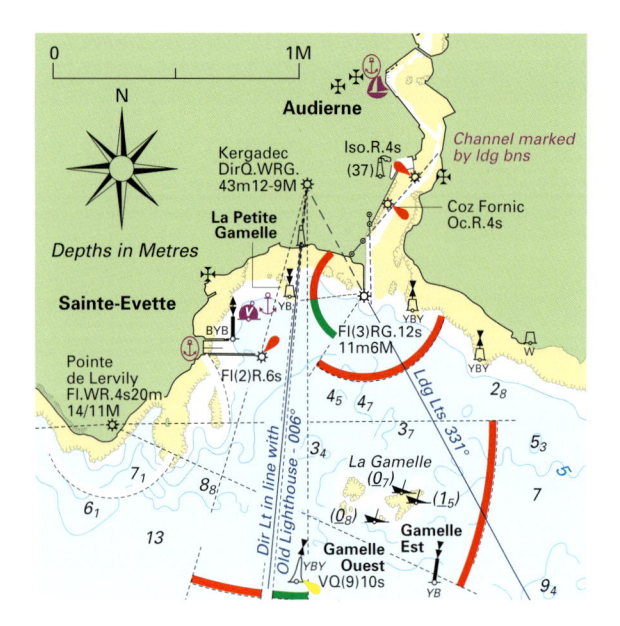

bearing right away to Douarnenez. But then we spotted a Breton gaff cutter under full sail heading the same way as us and confidence was restored.

We were abeam Tévennec at about 1630 as the stream was dwindling to nothing. With rising anticipation we reached on southwards over water that was now beginning to lump and swirl. The iconic trio of the old, grey La Vieille lighthouse perched high on its rock, the enormous wasp-striped westerly cardinal beacon La Plate and the Pointe du Raz semaphore tower on the headland above held us in awe as *Wild Bird* picked up speed on the new ebb, slewing and sliding through the bubbling overfalls. And then we were through – the wasp had missed its sting! The crew was jubilant and with light spirits we bore right away and ran gently along the coast towards Audierne. Gybing round inside La Gamelle, we headed up into Sainte Evette. The moorings were busy so we dropped anchor outside them. It was exactly 13 hours and just under 60 miles since we had left our mooring and we felt we had come through into a new, softer and sunnier world of southern Brittany. It was time to celebrate!

Looking E at La Vieille lighthouse on left, La Plate west cardinal beacon on right and Pte du Raz semaphore in middle beyond
Nick Chavasse

WHY VISIT?

Given sufficient tide, wind and stamina it is certainly possible to clear both tidal gates in a single passage, and there is some satisfaction in that. However, if you do that you will miss plenty of gems.

The Chenal du Four is flanked by Île d'Ouessant (Ushant) and Île Molène in the west and mainland France in the east. In settled weather, Ushant and Molène are well worth visiting, although be warned about the dangerous overfalls on the northwest side of Ushant, near Nividic. Île Molène deserves special mention because of its solitude and fine sandy beaches. It is also where on a foggy night in June 1896 the SS *Drummond Castle*, was shipwrecked on Les Pierres Vertes, 3M southwest of Molène. Of the 400 persons on board only three survived. There is a small museum on the island dedicated to this tragic loss.

On the mainland, there is the scenic harbour of L'Aber-Ildut, with a new marina built in 2018, and the fishing port of Le Conquet. If you wondered where CROSS Corsen is, having heard

Rites of Passage

L'ABERWRAC'H TO AUDIERNE

it endlessly on Channel 16, then ponder no longer as it is to be found mid-way between these two ports.

The delights of Camaret and the Rade de Brest are not far from your course. Camaret makes an excellent first port of call and offers wonderful 'moules frites' to hungry crew. Two marinas in Brest offer the normal services, though space is hard to come by if your visit coincides with the Festival of Sail. More tranquil spots are to be found in the nearby rivers Aulne and Elorn where crew of all ages will enjoy the wonderful wildlife - a contrast to the old naval hulks rusting at anchor in the river on the way up to Chateaulin, a delightful Breton town.

Further south, before going through the Raz, the Baie de Douarnenez offers shelter at Morgat, on the northern side, and at Douarnenez, tucked into the southeastern corner and world famous for its biennial maritime festival. The festival sometimes combines with Brest's Festival of Sail, a thrilling sight.

As for the Chenal du Four, there is no need to go rushing on by the Île de Sein which offers a pleasant fair weather stop. The port de Sein is sheltered from the south and west. The island is famous for its heroes when the entire male population left for England in their fishing boats to join the Free French during the Second World War. Nowadays a large number of lifeboat men come from the island.

Once clear of the Raz de Sein, past Audierne and on beyond Penmarch Point, it is often said that the weather becomes warmer. But this might be down to the holiday feel of well-known resorts like Bénodet or Concarneau and the turquoise waters of the Îles de Glénan ... but they are for another day.

In settled weather Île de Sein is an interesting place to explore
Shutterstock/ Synto

The moorings and anchorage at Ste Evette with the Audierne entrance channel beyond
Nick Chavasse

Rites of Passage 77

9 CHENAL DU FOUR AND RAZ DE SEIN

TIDAL STREAMS
The figures shown against the arrows are the mean rates at springs and neaps in tenths of a knot.
Thus 15,07 -
mean springs rate 1·5 knots, mean neaps rate 0·7 knots

IMRAY TIDES PLANNER
Imray Tides Planner app is a useful planning tool. Download from the App Store or Google Play.

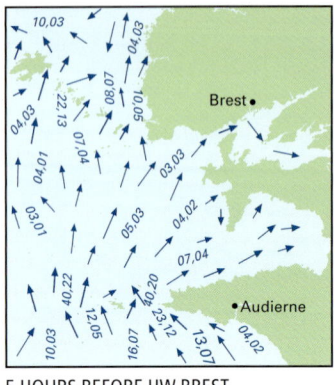

5 HOURS BEFORE HW BREST

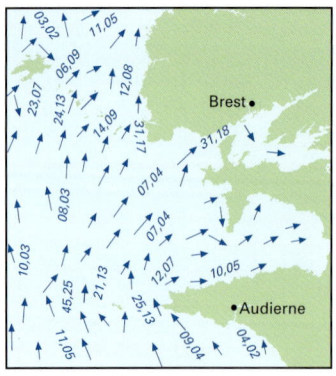

4 HOURS BEFORE HW BREST

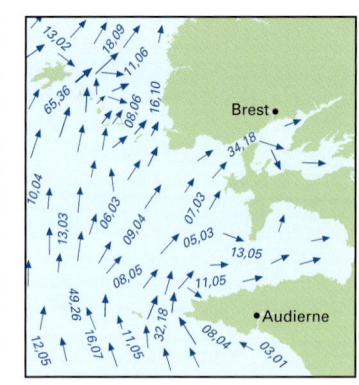

3 HOURS BEFORE HW BREST

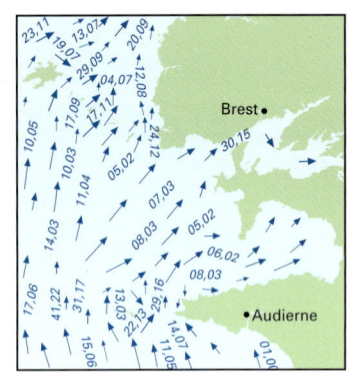

2 HOURS BEFORE HW BREST

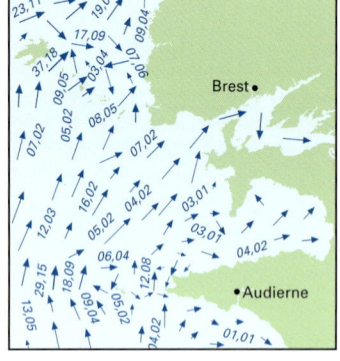

1 HOUR BEFORE HW BREST

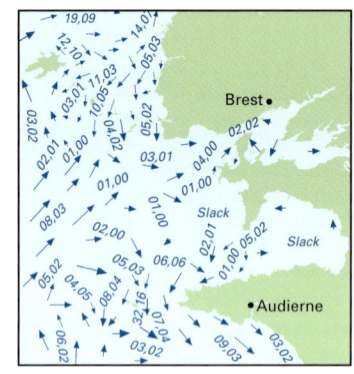

HW BREST

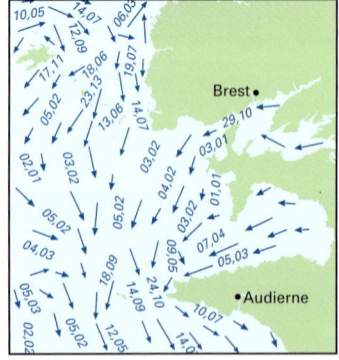

1 HOUR AFTER HW BREST

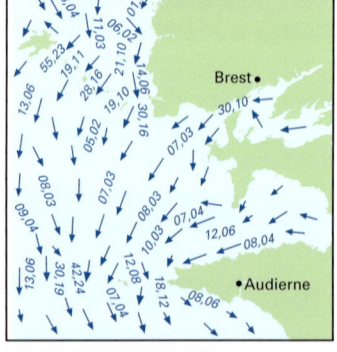

2 HOURS AFTER HW BREST

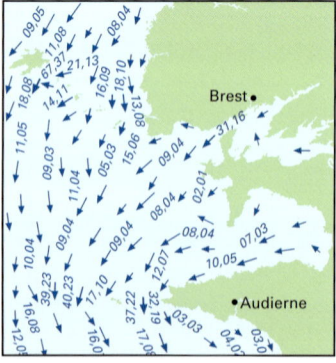

3 HOURS AFTER HW BREST

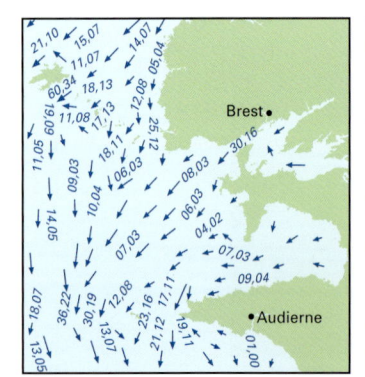

4 HOURS AFTER HW BREST

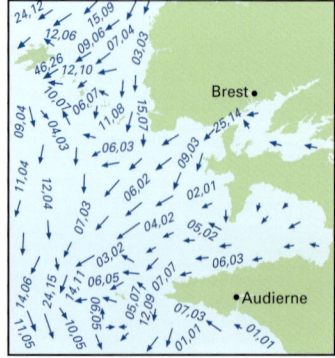

5 HOURS AFTER HW BREST

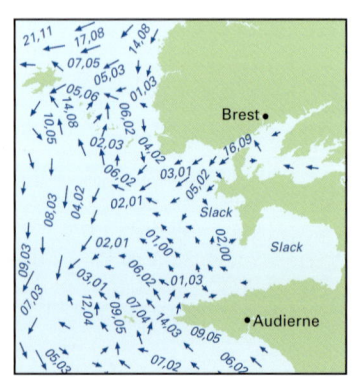

6 HOURS AFTER HW BREST

Rites of Passage

L'ABERWRAC'H TO AUDIERNE

Looking across Molène to the Chenal du Four beyond
Nick Chavasse

About the author

NICK CHAVASSE MBE was brought up sailing dinghies in the Helford River and then graduated to yachts during a first career in the Army. After retiring from a second career in marketing, he took on the authorship of the Royal Cruising Club Pilotage Foundation's *Atlantic France* (2nd edition), which was published in 2018. Nick sails with his family on *Wild Bird*, a Bowman 40. In addition to detailed research cruises along the Atlantic coast of France, he has sailed to the Azores, and in Scotland, the Baltic and the Med. Nick is a cruising instructor and the current Vice Commodore of The Royal Cruising Club.

Imray books and charts

Atlantic France
Ouessant to the Spanish Border
Nick Chavasse / Royal Cruising Club Pilotage Foundation (Imray)

The authoritative cruising companion for this long and varied coastline with its sometimes-daunting tides and currents ... welcomed both by first-time visitors to the region and by old hands who are revisiting their favourite haunts.

Chart packs (paper and digital)
2510 North Brittany

Passage charts
C36	Ile D'Ouessant to Raz de Seine	1:80,000
C37	Raz de Seine to Benodet	1:80,000
C35	C35 Baie de Morlaix to L'Aber-Ildut	1:75,000

Imray Digital
FRI   Bay of Biscay

Rites of Passage

Around Cape Wrath

Hugh Stewart

STROMNESS TO EAST LOCH TARBERT

'A sunny place for shady people' is how Somerset Maugham once described Monaco. Orkney is the opposite; a shady place for sunny people. Orcadians are some of the friendliest folk you will encounter, and we had been enjoying their warm hospitality to the tunes of many a fiddle band in the Folk Music Festival, washed down with a dram or two of Highland Park. We had also visited the amazing 5,000-year-old Skara Brae Neolithic settlement and the museum dedicated to North West Passage explorer John Rae. It's difficult to leave Orkney, it has a magnetic pull, but now it was time to set sail for the Western Isles, via Cape Wrath.

Our yacht was our 1960's designed, Viking manufactured, 33ft Hallberg Mistral, *Mikara*, a strongly-built composite with wooden superstructure on a GRP hull. I was sailing her with my wife Wendy. The three of us have sailed many miles together but rounding Cape Wrath still brought a frisson of foreboding. The very name, Cape Wrath, conjures up images of Norse gods hurling thunderbolts at ill-prepared yachtsmen. The name is indeed Norse but derives from the word 'hvarf' meaning simply 'turning point'. Thankfully, treated with respect it proved to be free of thunderbolts, even in unhelpful weather.

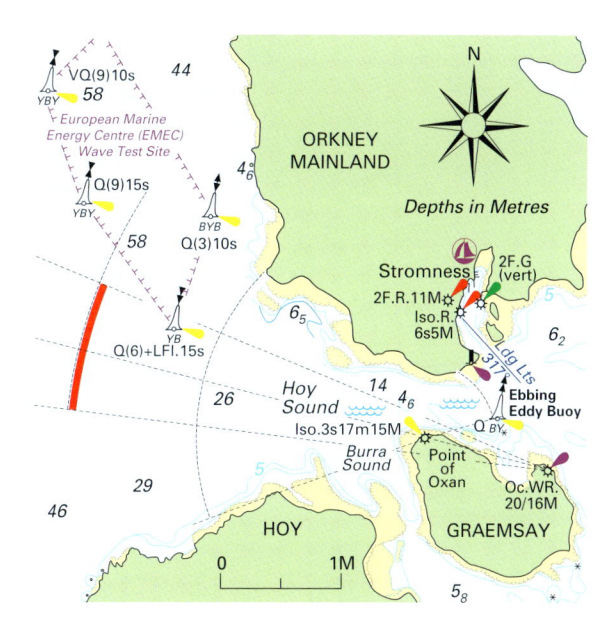

In an ideal world we'd have waited for a soldier's wind which would allow a direct passage of about 112 miles from Orkney to Stornoway on Lewis; achievable in 24 hours, and in summer mostly in daylight. But diaries dictated timing and we might have waited forever. The predominant wind is the WSW which has blown over 2,000 Atlantic miles to get there, so even in summer months there's a 50 percent chance of Force 5 or

Opposite
Orkney Yole and Graemsay lighthouse
Elinor Cole

Below
Stromness marina, Orkney, with Scapa Flow beyond
Elinor Cole

Rites of Passage

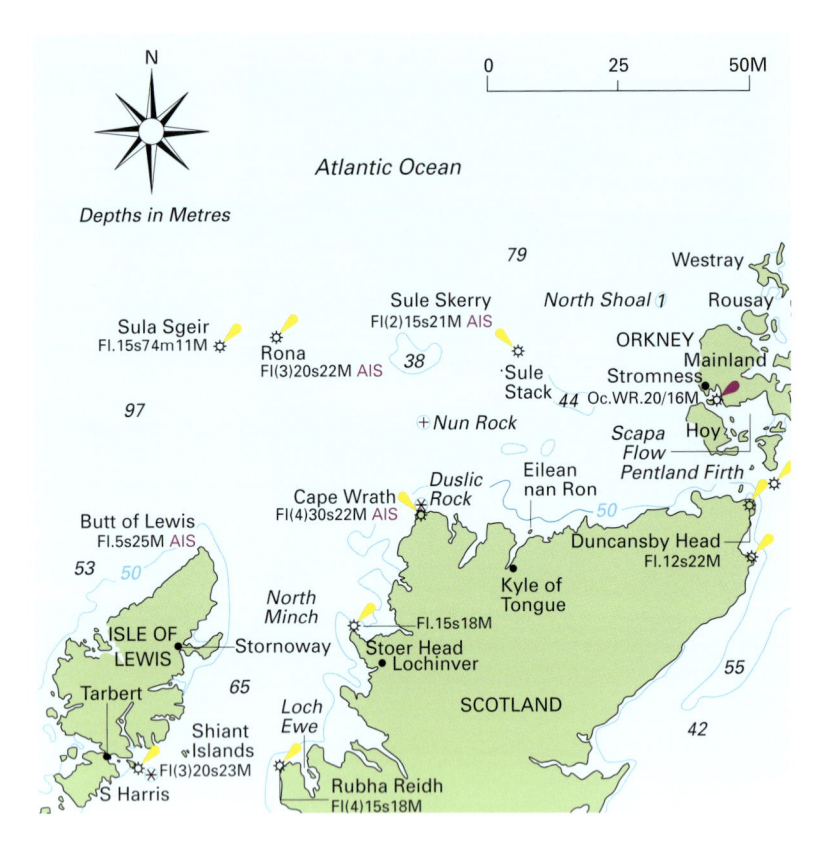

AROUND CAPE WRATH

PASSAGE PLANNER
Departure from Stromness

Standard Port Wick

| HWS | –0225 | HWN | –0135 |
| LWS | –0205 | LWN | –0205 |

| MHWS | MHWN | MLWN | MLWS |
| +0·1m | –0·1m | 0·0m | 0·0m |

Monitor wind and sea state forecasts very carefully as conditions can change rapidly. Cape Wrath is exposed to W and N and in strong NW through NE winds dangerous seas can build quickly.

Westwards from Stromness: Leave 30 minutes before the end of the ebb to avoid overfalls in the Sound of Hoy. The entrance to Eilean nan Ron anchorage in Kyle of Tongue is very narrow but straightforward by day. At night Loch Eriboll anchorages are preferable. Rounding Cape Wrath (Fl(4)W30s122m22M AIS), keep 3–5M offshore. In very settled conditions you can pass close inshore, but beware Duslic Rock (dries 3·4m), 7 cables NE of the lighthouse. The W-going stream off Cape Wrath begins at +0230 Ullapool.

East of Cape Wrath and extending 4M out, there is a live firing range - check for live firing times.

Cape Wrath with Duslic Rock at far right
Shutterstock / Dejonckheere

above and the likelihood of a gale. Our forecast was WSW Force 5–6; bang on the nose.

We were two days short of neaps but, even so, Orcadian tides still sluice between islands at a fearsome rate. We cast off from Stromness to time our passage through the Sound of Hoy at the last of the ebb, thereby avoiding the overfalls which are savage with wind against tide. The price for this was starting our voyage with a morale-threatening foul tide, but a bacon roll soon overcame that.

Our zig-zag plot looked like a goat track up a precipitous mountain as we tacked to and fro. Our target was Loch Eriboll, offering a selection of sheltered anchorages and only 15 miles from Cape Wrath, so perfect for timing the turn to avoid thunderbolts. Sadly, that was not to be. Our slow beating progress meant we had either

Rites of Passage

Suilven rears above the village of Lochinver
Shutterstock
John Roberts

to press on through the night or settle for something nearer. The only practical choice was Kyle of Tongue. The Clyde Cruising Club *Sailing Directions* describe a snug anchorage at Eilean nan Ron but by the time we reached the island near midnight it was pitch dark. I wouldn't recommend weaving through the rocks in the narrow entrance without full use of Mk I Eyeball, so we anchored in the lee of the island in 15m. The rule in Scotland, to carry at least 60m of chain, is for good reason. The following morning we could see into the recommended anchorage – ideal for next time!

Our next hurdle was still Cape Wrath. Except in calm conditions the advice is to keep well offshore. The WSW wind and tide set us a safe 6M north of the cape and our passage was lumpy but manageable. Then, having rounded the cape, we fully expected to turn downhill to enjoy a beam reach. No chance! Although we hadn't been struck by thunderbolts, we had clearly incurred some wrath as the wind backed to SW just as we altered course. More zig-zag goat tracks under two reefs!

The *Sailing Directions* describe some 31 anchorages between Cape Wrath and Loch Inver, so one could cheerfully linger in just this area: as Ronald Faux wrote in *The West: A Sailing Companion to the West Coast of Scotland: Gigha to Cape Wrath*, (second hand copies available online) 'This coastline has been described as the last true wilderness in Europe, [...] an emptiness filled with the sound and colour of the sea and hills, the wild din of black-backs and guillemots, razor bills and Arctic terns, and the eternal rhythm of the ocean.' Sadly, we needed modern refinement in the shape of gas. Having spent most of the season in Norway where fittings are different, and because the only Calor gas in Orkney is on a distant industrial estate, we had less than a sniff left. We had been cooking on our wonderful Cobb barbecue until an unfortunate crew communications confusion led to the ocean depths becoming host to the critical part. So, our destination was Loch Inver, where gas could be found in a fishing harbour with a dramatic backdrop of the sugar loaf mountain Suilven. On arrival, we decided against a climb of Suilven and instead opted for the easier reward of sipping its inspirational ale as our reward for having bagged our cape.

A pint of Suilven to celebrate bagging our cape
Hugh Stewart

Rites of Passage 83

10 AROUND CAPE WRATH

PASSAGE PLANNER
Arrival at East Loch Tarbert

Standard Port Stornoway

| HWS | −0010 | HWN | −0025 |
| LWS | −0010 | LWN | −0020 |

MHWS	MHWN	MLWN	MLWS
+0·2m	0·0m	+0·1m	+0·1m

South of Cape Wrath there are many anchorages and two harbours: The Bodha Ceann Na Seil shoal in Loch Inchard is marked with a lit NCB and the entrance is well lit. Continuing SW down the coast, strong wind against tide can cause bad seas off Point of Stoer, the headland N of Loch Inver. Entering Loch Inver from N, take care to avoid the drying Bo Caolas rocks NE of Soyea I. Glas Leac rock marks the final approach to Loch Inver and has a sector light. Loch Ewe offers a number of anchorages with shelter from different directions. East Loch Tarbert may be approached to N of Scalpay Island if air draft is less than 20m, this being the clearance under the bridge from North Harris. Larger yachts must route S of Scalpay.

Scalpay North Harbour has a pontoon or anchor off the pier, good shelter; Tarbert is 3M WNW of Scalpay, either use the pontoon or anchor WSW of ferry pier.

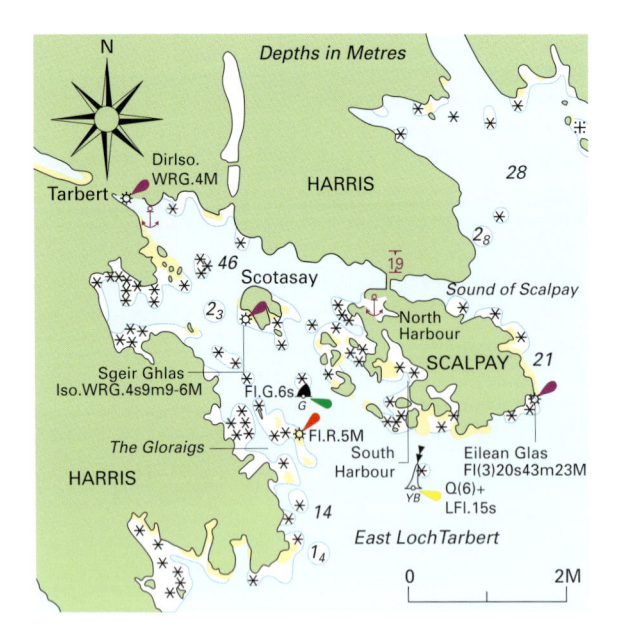

One of the joys of the west coast is changeable weather. It can be blowing a hooley with sheeting rain one day then be gentle breezes and sunshine the next. So it was, and the following day we enjoyed a lovely sail south in a NNW Force 4 to Loch Ewe, famous as an assembly point for the Second World War Arctic Convoys. Loch Ewe also boasts a beautiful anchorage adjacent to the gardens of Inverewe House. Although it's 7M to the head of the loch it's worthwhile, particularly if your mate is a keen gardener!

From gardening to high fashion; our final destination was East Loch Tarbert on Harris to buy tweed. The distinguishing feature of Harris Tweed is that, without even a nod towards improving productivity, it must be made in the weaver's private home using a traditional loom. This makes it rare. Indeed, this rarity leaves all other tweeds in the shade. Aside from this it is an excellent candidate for standing a watch in a gale. So, with this in mind, we beat out of Loch Ewe and then enjoyed a lovely reach to the Shiant

The lovely gardens at Inverewe House
Hugh Stewart

84 Rites of Passage

Islands, where we paused to watch puffins before continuing on to the stunning scenery of Tarbert.

We'd completed a challenging rounding of Cape Wrath and that in itself felt something of an achievement. But we had also experienced the culture and warmth of Orkney, felt the rhythm of the ocean, seen the changing faces of the Atlantic weather against towering coastal backdrops, and witnessed sunsets to make Turner rise again. Now the Western Isles lay at our doorstep. Life doesn't get much better.

WHY VISIT THE WESTERN ISLES?

The technical term for the Western Isles is the Outer Hebrides. Anything with Outer in its name inspires awe - Outer Space, the fluid Outer Core of the earth. The Hebrides are in that league. They're certainly awe-inspiring for the sailor: just look at the Sound of Harris, strewn with tiny islands and drying rocks, or the isolated archipelago of St Kilda, rising 432m out of the sea. So much scope for adventure.

But they also appeal to the senses: the sight of scintillating scenery that has so inspired artists; the sounds of swirling seabirds; the touch of seaweed, heather, rock; the taste of freshly caught cockles and crabs, and the smells - lichen, peat, melting tarmac in the sweltering sun, and of course the sea. Each person will have their own Western Isles best sense. For me it's the sounds. All that rich Gaelic heritage, the feeling of community and the natural landscape come together in the music of the Hebrides. That and the clacking of the looms.

The Western Isles are 120M tip to toe. When you arrive off Harris, roughly a third of the way south, you're at a T-junction. You could turn right to Stornoway, home each July to the Hebridean Celtic Festival. Or you could turn left and sail to the toe - Barra Head and Mingulay, made famous in the eponymous song written by Hugh Roberton in the 1930s:

Hill you ho, boys; Let her go, boys;
Bring her head round, now all together.
Hill you ho, boys; Let her go, boys;
Sailing home, home to Mingulay.

The moment you hear that beautiful lilting tune you're in that boat letting her go as the spume flies by.

Or you could go straight on, through the Sound of Harris to the white-sand beaches of the West Coast or the compelling sadness of St Kilda, 55M further W.

So that's 'Why the Western Isles'. But why North Harris as the landfall? In truth it was partly because the wind took us there. But there were other reasons - the search for Harris Tweed, with its award-winning advertising slogan '*From the land comes the cloth*', derived from an old Gaelic saying. Also the chance to visit the Shiant Islands. Aside from being picturesque and teeming with birdlife, they were once home to less welcome wildlife in the shape of rats who had landed from stranded ships. Compton McKenzie, author of the delightful Whisky Galore, owned the islands and he and his two brothers-in-law set out to deal with the rats, sailing to the Shiants armed with tins of arsenic. When they'd spread the poison they realised it was on their clothes so they lit a fire and burned them. Under cover of darkness they sailed back and crept into East Loch Tarbert but an old cailleach (lady) spotted them from her window and exclaimed '*I've just seen the MacSween boys running past in clothes that need a lot of ironing!*'. Thunderbolts were no doubt unleashed.

Just like Orkney, the Western Isles is populated by the friendliest of people. Maybe it's the frequent periods of highly inhospitable weather that draw the community together. In any case, both offer sailing that is challenging and rewarding in equal measure.

Tranquil waters at the head of Loch Ewe
Hugh Stewart

10 AROUND CAPE WRATH

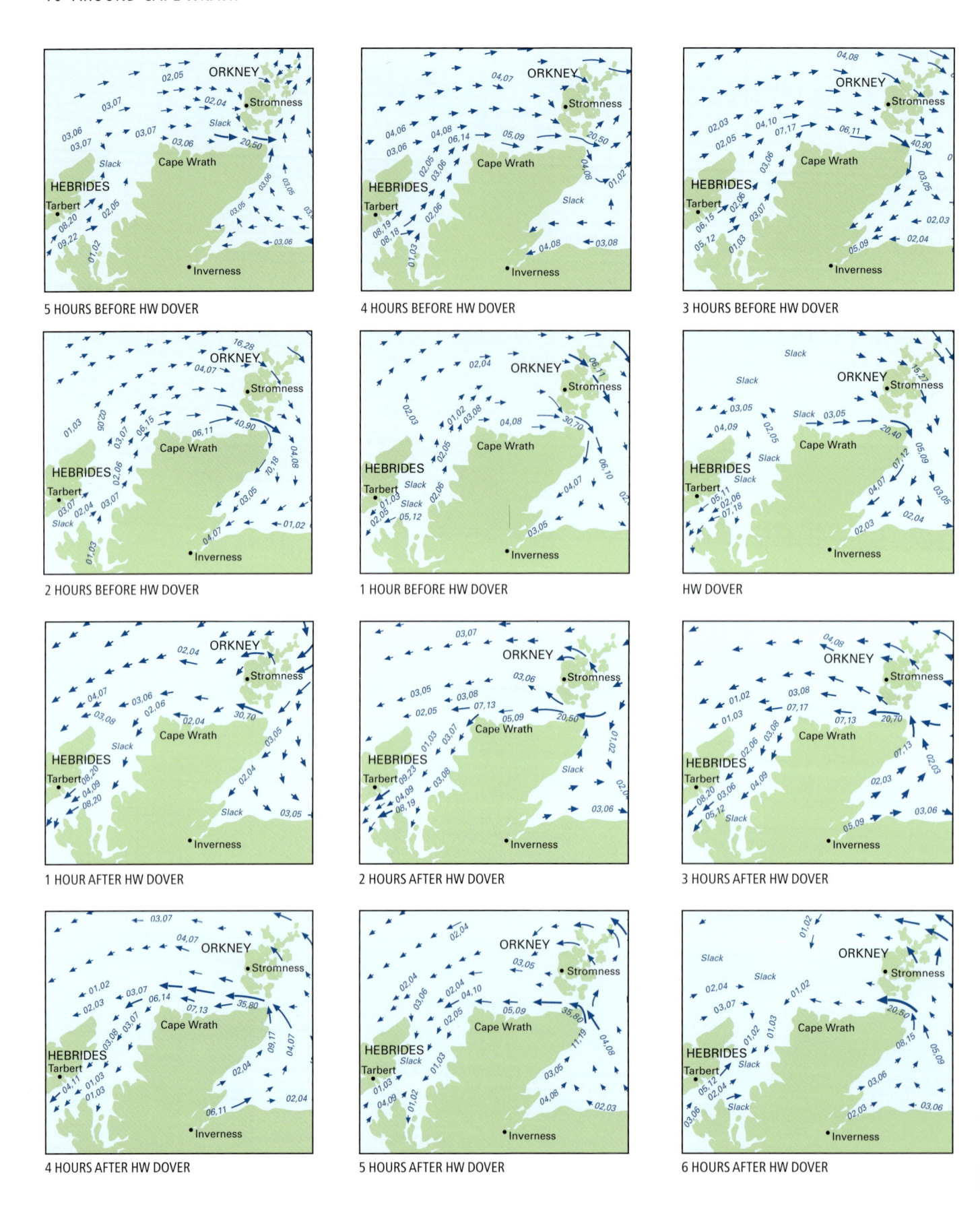

5 HOURS BEFORE HW DOVER

4 HOURS BEFORE HW DOVER

3 HOURS BEFORE HW DOVER

2 HOURS BEFORE HW DOVER

1 HOUR BEFORE HW DOVER

HW DOVER

1 HOUR AFTER HW DOVER

2 HOURS AFTER HW DOVER

3 HOURS AFTER HW DOVER

4 HOURS AFTER HW DOVER

5 HOURS AFTER HW DOVER

6 HOURS AFTER HW DOVER

TIDAL STREAMS

The figures shown against the arrows are the mean rates at neaps and springs in tenths of a knot. Thus 07,15 - mean neaps rate 0·7 knots, mean springs rate 1·5 knots

IMRAY TIDES PLANNER

Imray Tides Planner app is a useful planning tool. Download from the App Store or Google Play.

86 Rites of Passage

Wizard Pool, Loch Skipport, South Uist
Hugh Stewart

About the author

HUGH STEWART started sailing after he joined the Royal Naval Reserve and was lined up as crew for offshore races. Family circumstances then dictated dinghy sailing but he sought adventure with a couple of Hobie Cats. He bought *Mikara*, a 33ft Hallberg Mistral, 16 years ago and he and his wife Wendy have cruised extensively in France, Holland, Scandinavia and particularly in Scotland where *Mikara* is kept. They have twice circumnavigated Britain, on the second occasion the long way via Norway, Shetland and Orkney.

Imray books and charts

Orkney and Shetland
Clyde Cruising Club Sailing Directions (Imray)

This comprehensive guide to Orkney and Shetland, which includes Fair Isle, also covers the 'jumping off' harbours on south side of the Pentland Firth and the mainland coast of Scotland between Inverness and Cape Wrath.

Ardnamurchan to Cape Wrath
Clyde Cruising Club Sailing Directions (Imray)

Covers the north section of the West Coast of Scotland from Ardnamurchan Point to Cape Wrath, including the whole of Skye and the Small Isles.

Outer Hebrides
Clyde Cruising Club Sailing Directions (Imray)

A comprehensive companion for small-boat visitors to this unspoilt area with its many secluded anchorages. Coverage begins in Barra Head and stretches northeast to East Lewis and west to the exposed Atlantic coast and the remote islands of the St Kilda group.

Cruising Scotland
Clyde Cruising Club (Imray)

This lavishly illustrated book has been designed as a companion to the Clyde Cruising Club's Sailing Directions and covers the Scottish west coast from the Clyde to Cape Wrath and all the outlying islands. Cruising Scotland provides additional information, points of interest and many photographs and is a fascinating and invaluable addition to the Club's publications. No yacht cruising the Scottish west coast should be without a copy.

Passage charts

C67 North Minch and Isle of Lewis	1:155,000
C68 Cape Wrath to Wick and the Orkney Islands	1:160,000
C80 British Isles	1:1 500 000

Imray Digital
ID30 West Britain and Ireland

Across the northern North Sea

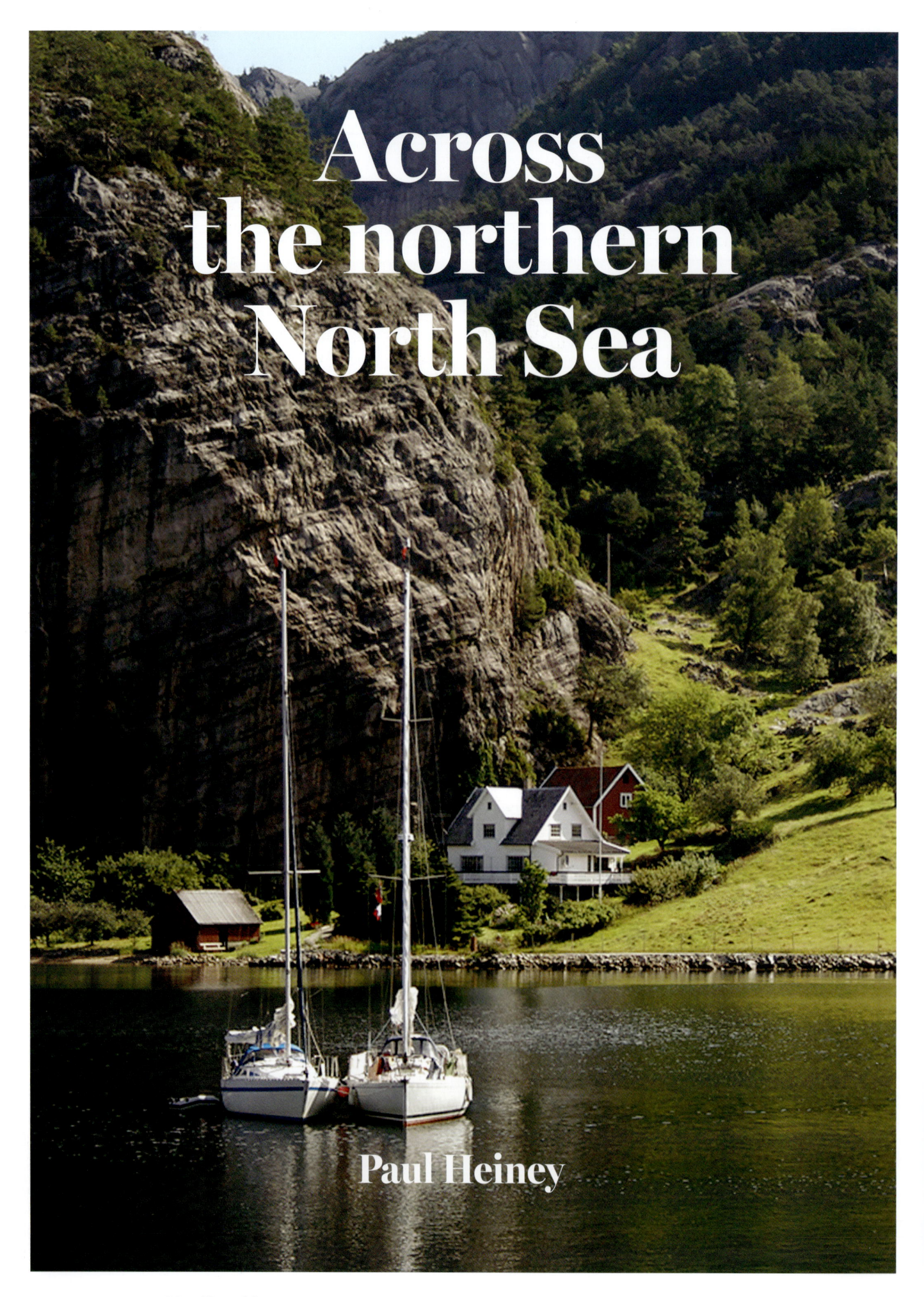

Paul Heiney

There's no law that says a rite of passage has to be easy. In fact, quite the reverse. It is supposed to mark a turning point in your life where you open your eyes to new appreciations and understandings. My passage from Lerwick to Bergen certainly did that.

It was some years ago when we owned a venerable wooden yawl; graceful and speedy, but built in the early '60s when long, open water passages were less common. Consequently, she had little fuel capacity and, remarkably, no fresh water tanks at all. So, I fitted one: a huge black rubber-like bladder which lurked up the counter, flopping back and forth like a stranded whale. I little appreciated the mistake I had made, but this apparently straightforward passage was soon to point out the error of my ways.

The navigation should have been no problem. It was roughly 200 miles on a course pretty much due east. Given the prevailing weather is from the west, what could possibly go wrong? I had sailed up the east coast of England the previous summer in easy weather, overwintered at the hospitable Malakoff shipyard in Lerwick, and with a forecast that was not perfect, but do-able, we left the comforting enclosure of the small boat harbour and hoisted full sail to make our way northwards up the sound between Lerwick and Bressay. Before we were past Easter Rova Head (Fl(3)WRG), and not even in the open sea, the crew was sick. This was, however, a mere rehearsal for what he was later to endure.

Mindful that this is some years ago, I had just replaced an uncertain Decca navigator with a GPS and was still marvelling at what an aid this was. But I had no radar, and AIS was still 20 years away. However, I had a good pair of eyes, a hand-bearing compass, and a decent paper chart which showed me the positions of the oil and gas fields which were rapidly proliferating in those parts. I also carried a set of somewhat scary Norwegian charts which reminded me how intricate their coastline was, and how easy it would be to get lost: each chart showed at least a score of offshore islands, mostly unpronounceable. How would I ever know which was which?

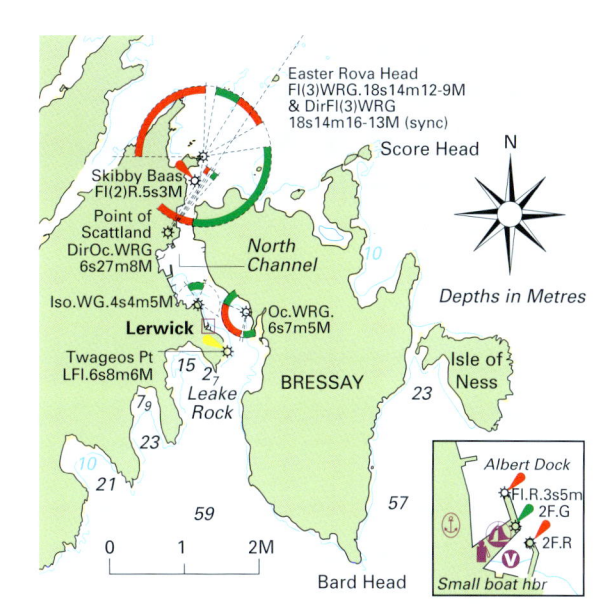

Also lacking in those days was up-to-date weather forecasting so I was sailing on the basis of a BBC shipping forecast, glued to Fair Isle, Viking and North Utsire, which were the areas we would be sailing through. They were talking of westerly Force 5 or 6 at the time we left. I felt happy with that for a downwind passage.

Opposite
Lysefjord
David Lomax

Below
Lerwick small boat harbour
*Shutterstock
Alan Morris*

Rites of Passage 89

PASSAGE PLANNER
Departure from Lerwick

Standard Port Lerwick

Lerwick to Bergen is the shortest route between the UK and Norway, 210 miles including 20 miles up the fjords inside the protection of Sotra Island. Monitor the wind and swell patterns before departure and try to find a moderate window of winds and seas.

The main hazards are the oil platforms in the North Sea; a careful lookout should also be kept for fishing boats.

Lerwick North channel is well marked but narrow and busy with commercial vessels including the ferry which runs between Lerwick and Bressay. Tidal streams run North from +0130 HW Lerwick (2kn at Springs).

There is some useful information at www.shetlandmarinas.com and www.lerwick-harbour.co.uk/yachts, and for weather in the North Sea; www.yr.no

---

But 50 miles from Lerwick, I began feeling less comfortable as the wind freshened and the seas rose. I had no instruments, but it felt more than Force 6 to me and the genoa was quickly rolled to a scrap. Ear glued to a feeble transistor radio, amidst a distant, crackling cricket commentary came a warning of Force 7 possibly 8. The seas were now gathering and the crew was in a near coma.

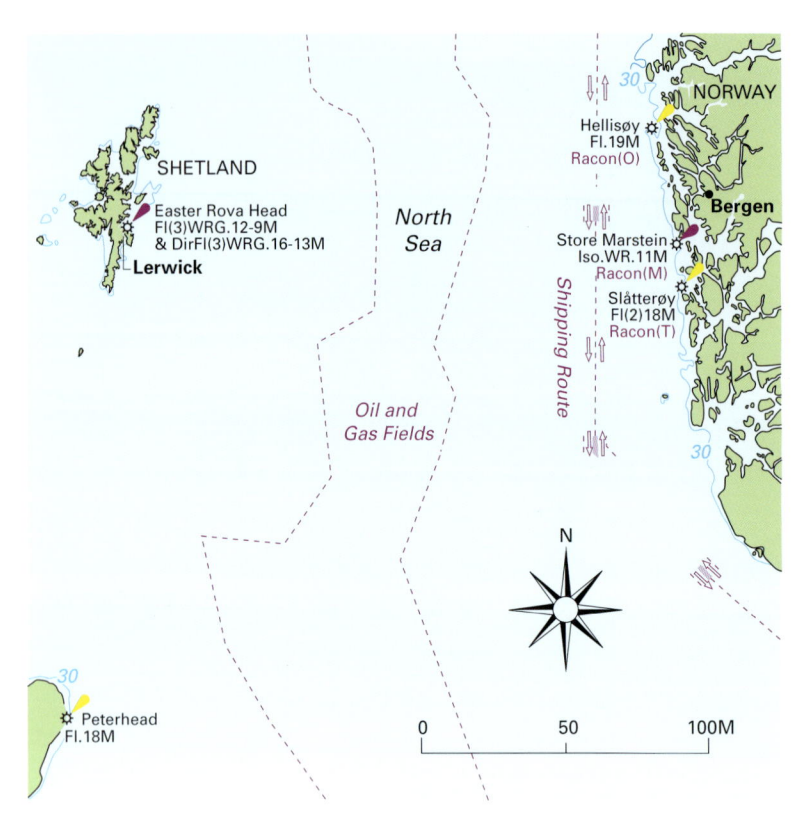

Spectacular scenery in Hardangerfjord
Judy Lomax

There was no possibility of turning back, the passage had to be completed, and over the next couple of hours I hastily learnt the principles of waypoint navigation using GPS. It seemed like a blessing from heaven. For the first time in my sailing career, I actually knew where I was and what I was pointing at! I made tea and could just about keep down a ham sandwich. The crew, who could normally swallow an entire pasty in one gulp, declined.

Lack of complete darkness is one advantage of Norwegian summer sailing. The estimated time of arrival (ETA), a novel concept, turned out to

Stabben lighthouse
Judy Lomax

be a surprise gift from that wondrous little GPS, and although all the indications were that I would be arriving in the lengthy daylight hours, I set a course for the 1.5-mile gap between the small islands of Tekslo (Fl.WRG 5s 8M) and Marstein (Iso WR. 4s 11M) which light the entrance into the Korsfjorden.

I reckoned that from Tekslo I would be in the comparative shelter of the Korsfjorden, and then in total shelter on the final dog leg up to Bergen. So I pressed on with confidence, my spirit dented only by persistent rain and the moan of a haunting wind, underscored by a groaning crew.

With about 60 miles to go, the freshwater bladder started to make its presence felt. It was a serious mistake, which any half competent boat builder would have recognised, to place so much weight so far aft in a not very buoyant counter. My boat's rear end had grace and real beauty, a tribute to the wooden boatbuilder's craft, but it didn't see any reason to rise up as the waves approached, and the weight of the heavy water bladder wasn't helping. The following seas had started to break into the cockpit from where they drained straight into the bilge, as was common in boats of that era.

I seriously believed we were going to sink and thought I ought to mention this. Like Lazarus, the ashen-faced crew rose from his bunk and started to pump with the vigour of a man living through the last day of his life – and still 40 miles to shelter.

Utsire
David Lomax

11 ACROSS THE NORTHERN NORTH SEA

Arrival at Bergen

The Norwegian coast is steep-to and the main channels are well marked and deep. The lead to Bergen is up Korsfjorden and Raunefjorden, passing either side of Bjørøyna.

Tidal flow is generally less of a consideration on this coast, but the stream runs strongly through Vatlestraum, N on the flood and S on the ebb. Once you are under the high (49m) Litla Sotra bridge you enter Byfjord, which takes you NE under the even higher (63m) Askøy bridge and round into Puddefjord and the final approach to Bergen.

Bergen harbour offers complete shelter, although a strong NW wind might create a chop, as can the wash from commercial vessels. Rafting up alongside the dock in Vågen is in the heart of the old harbour but be aware that berths here can be noisy.

Our landfall was shrouded by rain and wave, but the GPS had worked its miracle and the shelter of the Norwegian islands eventually wrapped themselves around us. The crew was restored to health as the sea flattened, the sailing once again a pleasure, and the sight of colourful and vibrant Bergen the final tonic. We moored alongside the picturesque Bryggen quay, on the northern side of Vågen, the old harbour, with multi-coloured warehouses now turned to shops, cafes and boutiques.

The former Hanseatic port is stuffed with history, accessed via its museums and art galleries. The city itself has a truly cosmopolitan feel and it has claimed to have more bookshops per head of population than any other city in the world, and all with an English section. Since it also seems to have a similar number of coffee shops, and if your idea of recovering from a passage is to while away the day sipping coffee while stuck into a good book, you will be well satisfied. But take a coat. It is famously the wettest place in Norway with rain reckoned to fall on 260 days of the year. I can testify to the truth of that. Vessel and crew had come through, but my rite of passage? What new understanding had I arrived at? Was it a new confidence bestowed by satellite navigation? Or that everyone should, at least once in their lives, own a beautiful old wooden boat, but not for very long.

But in case any of this puts you off, the return trip offered the lightest of breezes which enabled us to ghost across a flat sea propelled by a willing, elegant mizzen staysail. A magical trip under clear skies.

South Utsire
David Lomax

92 Rites of Passage

WHY VISIT?

Judy Lomax

Once upon a time, the Norse gods and giants hurled rocks of all shapes and sizes at each other. They stumped across the mountains in unrighteous indignation, creating fjords as winding as their angry wanderings, and as deep and steep as the cliffs and mountains above them. The rocks became islands and skerries, crinkly bits which provide shelter along almost the whole coast. Aided and abetted by glacial and volcanic action, the result is a wondrously complex coast, almost all within the shelter of islands of all sizes, shapes and heights.

Starting from Bergen, there is plenty of scope to explore both fjords and crinkly bits. Turn south for the Hardangerfjord, or north for the Sognefjord, both flowing from way inland between mountains and below glaciers. The scenery is spectacular to magnificent. A choice of routes weaves among large inshore islands between the fjords. This looks bewildering, but routes are well marked, Norwegian charts are accurate, and GPS can be trusted. Gule sider (Yellow Pages) has an excellent app, På sjøen, which costs less than £15 a year.

The smaller outer islands were once tiny isolated communities as near the fishing grounds as possible in the days before engines. A few dozen, or at most a few hundred, inhabitants became thousands during the fishing season, living in simple wooden rorbua, now picturesque holiday accommodation. Even the smallest fishing harbours are well maintained, and mooring is usually cheaper in Norway than the UK, except in big town marinas. Anchoring is almost always free.

Among the many joys of cruising in Norway are the long hours of summer daylight, and not having to get up at unreasonable hours to catch the tide. In and near Bergen, there are nearly 19 hours of daylight in June and July, and the tidal range is only 1·22m. Both daylight hours and tidal range increase the further north one sails - or decrease to the south. The lack of significant tide makes for relaxed cruising – no need to set an alarm to catch the tide, no worrying about whether it is incoming or outgoing, or whether children can safely potter about in dinghies. It also simplifies anchoring; or mooring Norwegian-style alongside a rockface where the water is as deep as the rocks above are steep.

There is a common misconception that it is always cold in Norway, but it's possible to sail round North Cape in T-shirt weather. Between Bergen and Stavanger it can be so hot that swimming stops are needed in order to cool off – and the water is warmer than it ever is in Devon or Cornwall. In South Norway and the Oslofjord, the summer inshore sea temperature is often 20–26°C, and July heatwave air temperatures can reach into the high 20s and even low 30s.

It takes more than one summer to explore this most complex and beautiful coast. A few weeks out of Bergen might reach 115 miles north towards Statt – north of which the scenery and the sailing become even more rugged and wonderful; or 130 miles south to Stavanger and Ryfylke's large sheltered inland bay of islands and minor fjords, a perfect family cruising ground. That's without detours up fjords or among islands. There are plenty of places to leave a yacht over the winter, during which the west and north coasts remain ice-free. The gentler south coast and Oslofjord are within easy reach from Denmark or the west coast of Sweden or the Baltic, extending Norwegian cruising time beyond the permitted two years.

*Mooring Norwegian-style, Forlandsvågen
Judy Lomax*

11 ACROSS THE NORTHERN NORTH SEA

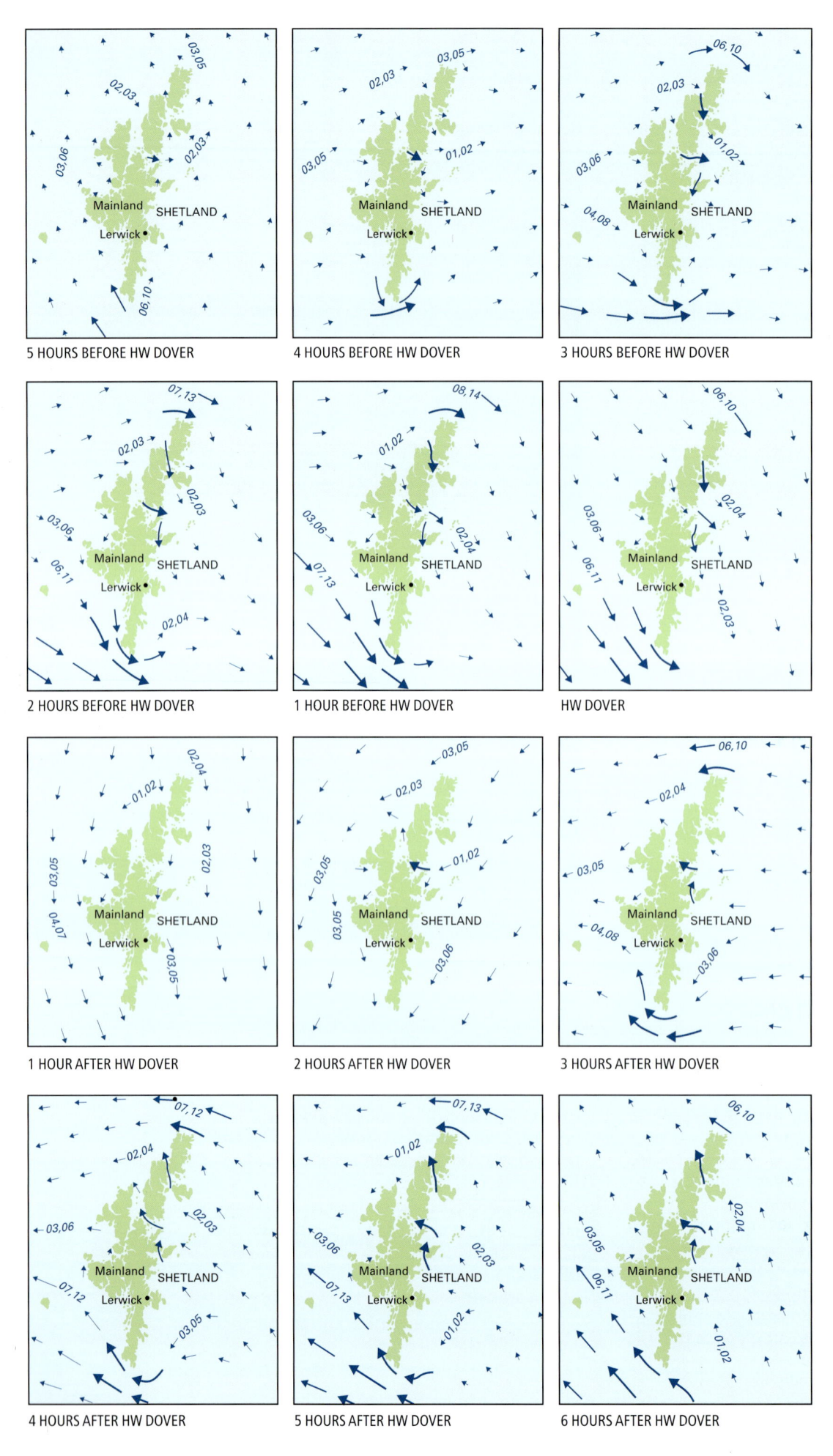

5 HOURS BEFORE HW DOVER

4 HOURS BEFORE HW DOVER

3 HOURS BEFORE HW DOVER

2 HOURS BEFORE HW DOVER

1 HOUR BEFORE HW DOVER

HW DOVER

1 HOUR AFTER HW DOVER

2 HOURS AFTER HW DOVER

3 HOURS AFTER HW DOVER

4 HOURS AFTER HW DOVER

5 HOURS AFTER HW DOVER

6 HOURS AFTER HW DOVER

TIDAL STREAMS

The figures shown against the arrows are the mean rates at neaps and springs in tenths of a knot. Thus 07,15 - mean neaps rate 0·7 knots, mean springs rate 1·5 knots

IMRAY TIDES PLANNER

Imray Tides Planner app is a useful planning tool. Download from the App Store or Google Play.

94 Rites of Passage

Uttoskavåg
Judy Lomax

About the author

PAUL HEINEY is a well-known writer and broadcaster and has been cruising widely for over four decades. In more recent years he has taken part in the Azores and Back Race (AZAB), the OSTAR and most recently sailed his Victoria 38, *Wild Song*, to Cape Horn and back, much of it singlehanded. He is the author of the Pilotage Foundation's *Ocean Sailing*, currently commodore of the Royal Cruising Club, and a Younger Brother of Trinity House.

Imray books and charts

Norway
Judy Lomax / Royal Cruising Club Pilotage Foundation (Imray)

This pilot from the RCC covers the long and complex coast of Norway, from the Swedish border in the Skagerrak to the Russian border, including the Lofoten and Vesterålen islands, the Arctic archipelago of Svalbard and the remote volcanic island of Jan Mayen.

Orkney and Shetland Islands
Clyde Cruising Club Sailing Directions (Imray)

This comprehensive guide to Orkney and Shetland, which includes Fair Isle, also covers the 'jumping off' harbours on south side of the Pentland Firth and the mainland coast of Scotland between Inverness and Cape Wrath.

Shetland Islands Pilot
Gordon Buchanan (Imray)

Gordon Buchanan knows the Shetland Islands from visits over many years and presents detailed pilotage information on reaching and cruising this delightful area.

Norwegian paper charts – Kartverket 021, 023
(Printed on demand from Imray)

Online charts at
www.kart.kystverket.no

To St Kilda and back

Mary Max

TARANSAY TO LOCHMADDY VIA ST KILDA

St Kilda has often been described as the edge of the world and it is easy to see why. The small archipelago of rocks and islands really does feel like a dot in the ocean. Miss St Kilda and the next stop is America!

It was early July and we had gathered at Loch Ewe to take over *Sai See* from my sister. *Sai See* is my parents' 40ft teak Sparkman and Stephens centreboard yawl. A lovely boat, both to look at and to sail, it has been part of our family for nearly 40 years. I had recently passed my Yachtmaster, but it was only my third time as skipper. On board with me were my husband-to-be, Daniel, and two friends from university.

We had arrived in a small hire car packed with luggage and provisions, with packets of crisps and Cup-a-Soup slotted into every available shelf and door pocket. It soon transpired that my sister and crew had almost run out of food and they somehow retained most of ours as they relieved us of the car and waved farewell.

The consequence of this sibling piracy was a need for a pub every evening. This dictated an excellent itinerary, and we had some memorable days of light wind sailing, energetically hoisting the spinnaker at every opportunity.

Before embarking on the long passage out to St Kilda we anchored for the night in Loch na h-Uidhe on the south side of Taransay. There's no pub, but it is a lovely anchorage in quiet weather and was a perfect jumping off point.

Our forecast looked good. N or NW 4 or 5, decreasing over the next 48 hours. Perfect. We were set to go. Daniel and I weighed anchor and set sail at first light, leaving our crewmates dead to the world down below. It was an absolutely stunning start to the day. We watched the sun rise over Taransay as we sailed out on a dead run under main, mizzen and jib in a few gentle puffs of wind. As we cleared the island and headed up onto our course the wind came onto the starboard beam and we swapped the jib for the cruising chute. We were feeling satisfied with our quiet and seamless sail change but our efforts had not gone unnoticed and we were soon joined on deck by our crew bearing some very welcome tea and toast.

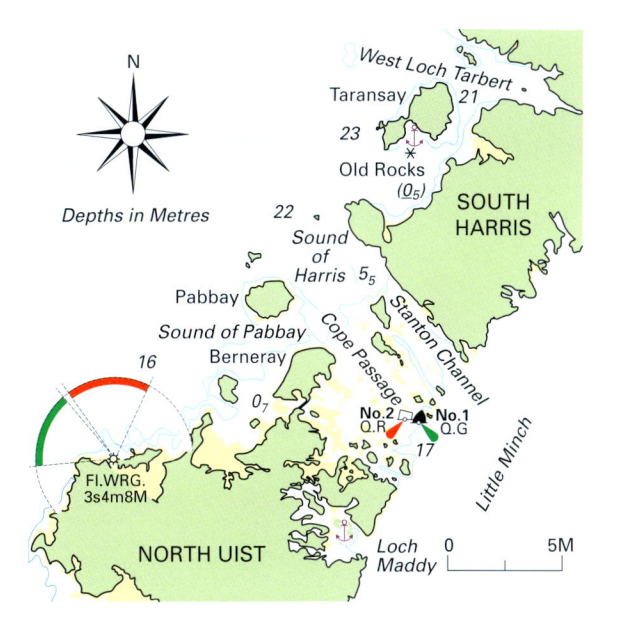

Once we had set up a watch system for the day we settled into a gentle rhythm, lazily watching the hours go by, with frequent interludes for more tea, toast and soup. The wind stayed fresh from the north with only a few moments of rain, and *Sai See* danced over the 55 miles to Village

Opposite
Stac an Armin,
Boreray
*Shutterstock
Corlaffra*

Below
Taransay
Clyde Cruising Club

Rites of Passage 97

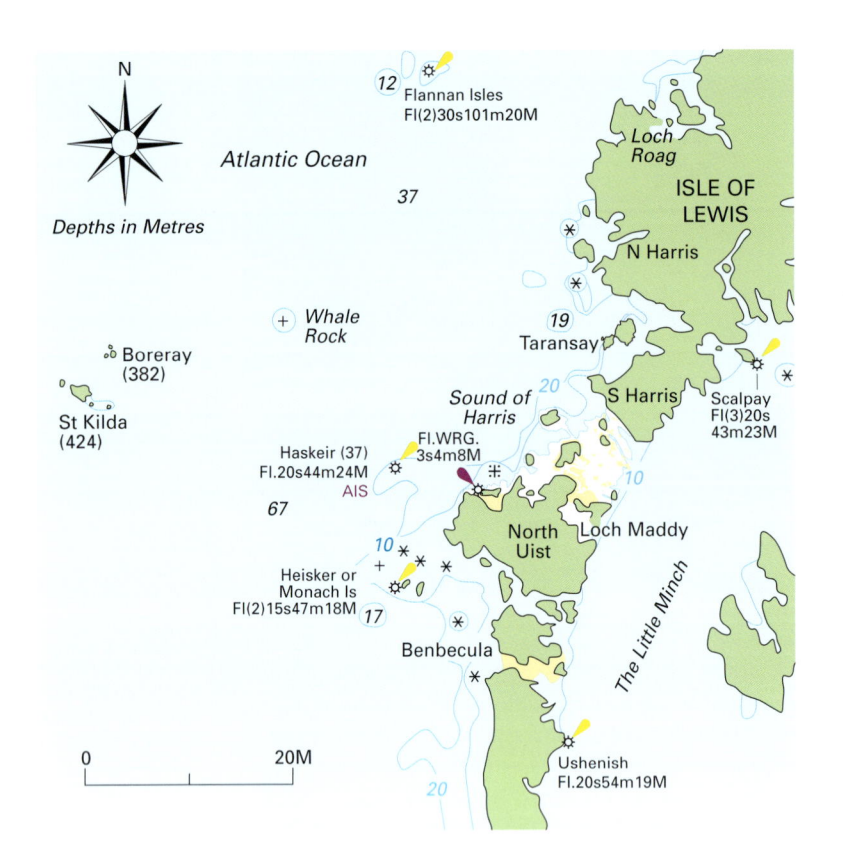

12 TO ST KILDA AND BACK

PASSAGE PLANNER
Departure from Taransay

West Loch Tarbert, Harris
Standard Port Stornoway
HW -0015   LW -0046
MHWS MHWN MLWN MLWS
-1·1m -0·9m -0·5m -0·0m

Taransay to St Kilda is a 50-mile passage, due west. The return passage to Berneray is a similar distance. A reasonably gentle tidal flow runs in a northerly and southerly direction, so the effect on your course is negligible over a 10-hour sail. The most important factor is the weather – this is a very exposed piece of water with frequent high seas.

The Atlantic coast of the Outer Hebrides has little shelter and in heavy weather conditions becomes dangerous in passages between the islands. This means that the necessary weather window is not just for the 50 miles getting to St Kilda, but also for the time spent there and a safe return passage. If conditions deteriorate make for Loch Roag on the west coast of Lewis. East Loch Roag, lit by Aird Laimishader and Greinam, is the only anchorage on the west side of the Outer Hebrides that is approachable at night.

Cope Passage through the Sound of Harris is not recommended without GPS or local knowledge. The alternative route via Stanton Channel is deeper and well marked but tides can run strongly in some sections (4 knots at springs).

Bay without us having to alter her sails at all. We read books, polished the brass and occupied ourselves with a few other maintenance jobs. We were all looking forward to our first sight of the islands, but the steep stacks of rock that rose above the horizon were even more magnificent than we had imagined.

There are no hazards in the entrance to the sweeping haven of Village Bay on the largest island, Hirta. We sailed gently on to the anchor in the north of the bay, as close in to the land, and the pub, as possible. However, our arrival at the Puff Inn revealed that they had run out of beer, so we were forced to sustain ourselves with their generous portions of whisky. Not surprisingly we stayed a while, and then continued the evening on board with the crew from a neighbouring German yacht.

St Kilda from North Uist on a clear day
Clyde Cruising Club

The next morning could best be described as decelerated! When we finally emerged into the blue sky we set off to investigate the *cleits* above the ruined village. There are an amazing 1,260 of these small, stone, turf-covered storage sheds on Hirta alone. Hirta is a fascinating island and the whole St Kilda group is a World Heritage Site. The resilience and self-sufficiency of the islanders

98   Rites of Passage

Arrival at St Kilda

Standard Port Stornoway
HW -0040   LW -0045
MHWS MHWN MLWN MLWS
-1·4m -1·1m -0·8m -0·3m

The islands can be seen from over 20 miles in good visibility, but at night the only lights are the leading lights with a range of 3 miles. There can be a strong tide rip across the mouth of Village Bay, creating overfalls in the channel between Levenish and Dun.

There is always some swell except during extended periods of calm. The anchorage at Village Bay is in 5-6m off the pier below the church, with good holding on hard sand. It is sheltered from N to W winds, but very open from NE-E-S. There is no other viable anchorage; Glen Bay, on the opposite side of the island, is subject to accelerated gusts of wind and is very deep and rocky.

Conditions can change rapidly. If you are caught out there is no option but to head back to the Outer Hebrides, whatever the conditions or time of day.

The main island is owned by National Trust for Scotland and leased to Scottish National Heritage and the Army. www.kilda.org.uk

Visitors should call *Kilda Warden* on VHF 12/16 on arrival.

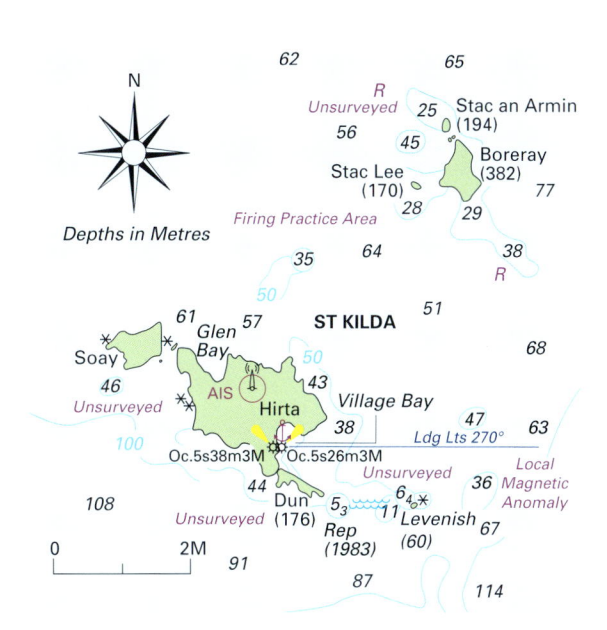

must have been extraordinary. They survived on a diet of sea birds, eggs, sheep and anything they could grow, such as barley and oats. The last of the islanders left in 1930.

We spent several hours exploring, taking in the spectacular views from the peak of Conachair (430m), despite the squadrons of dive-bombing skuas. A burst of rain signalled time to retreat and we headed back down. Another must on St Kilda is to take the dinghy across to the southern

Village Bay, St Kilda, looking south towards Dun Island
Shutterstock EvolvePhoto

Lochmaddy Marina
Clyde Cruising Club

Sai See in the islands
Mary Max

end of the bay and around Dun Island to see the puffins, and we didn't want to miss the chance. The crew eventually had to drag me away from the rafts of these lovely birds.

With the weather still holding, the following morning we called by the gannetry on Boreray. Witnessing the dense cloud of gannets swirling overhead in the bright sunshine is a sight not to be forgotten.

The moderate NW then sent us on our way on a satisfying broad reach, but it was not long before the wind began to fail us. We began to drift slower and slower until the last of the breeze deserted us entirely. But in good visibility in the glassy calm and with the tide under us, conditions for the Cope Passage would be favourable. Engine on, once we had identified Pabbay and Berneray, we used the GPS to navigate our way through the mass of reefs until we were spat out into the Little Minch.

We were keen to head to the Lochmaddy Hotel to celebrate, but we were to be disappointed. All the mooring buoys were occupied, and we ended up in the small anchorage between En Phail and Shealtragam. Daniel and I were dismayed at the prospect of having nothing to eat on board, but our luck had not yet run out and the crew disappeared down below and somehow rustled up a delicious three-course meal. It was a fitting end to a truly wonderful voyage.

TARANSAY TO LOCHMADDY VIA ST KILDA

St Kilda village and cleits
Clyde Cruising Club

The St Kilda northern gannet colony is the largest in the world
Shutterstock

WHY VISIT ST KILDA?

Of all the rites of passage in home waters this must surely qualify as one of the most challenging. Once you have committed to visiting St Kilda you are at the mercy of the Atlantic weather systems and, importantly, the ocean swell. There are some who have made it to the island, only to have to turn back without even making it ashore. But if the weather is right it is an unforgettable experience and you will be able to count yourself amongst the few who have arrived there 'on their own keel' to witness the extraordinary bird life and the remarkable history of human endeavour on the island.

12 TO ST KILDA AND BACK

5 HOURS BEFORE HW DOVER

4 HOURS BEFORE HW DOVER

3 HOURS BEFORE HW DOVER

2 HOURS BEFORE HW DOVER

1 HOUR BEFORE HW DOVER

HW DOVER

1 HOUR AFTER HW DOVER

2 HOURS AFTER HW DOVER

3 HOURS AFTER HW DOVER

4 HOURS AFTER HW DOVER

5 HOURS AFTER HW DOVER

6 HOURS AFTER HW DOVER

TIDAL STREAMS

The figures shown against the arrows are the mean rates at neaps and springs in tenths of a knot. Thus 07,15 - mean neaps rate 0·7 knots, mean springs rate 1·5 knots

IMRAY TIDES PLANNER

Imray Tides Planner app is a useful planning tool. Download from the App Store or Google Play.

102   Rites of Passage

TARANSAY TO LOCHMADDY VIA ST KILDA

Anchorage at Pabay Mor north, West Loch Roag
Clyde Cruising Club

About the author

MARY MAX has been sailing all of her life, initially with her parents on their 40ft Sparkman and Stephens yawl, *Sai See*. Childhood holidays were spent mostly in northern climes, including cruises to the Shetlands, Iceland and Norway. Mary began to skipper *Sai See* and spread her wings after gaining her RYA Yachtmaster, spending long summers on board with her friends and husband, Daniel, before adding their children to the crew. For the last 11 years she has cruised extensively around the west coast of Scotland with her family.

Imray books and charts

Outer Hebrides
Clyde Cruising Club Sailing Directions (Imray)
A comprehensive companion for small-boat visitors to this unspoilt area with its many secluded anchorages. Coverage begins in Barra Head and stretches northeast to East Lewis and west to the exposed Atlantic coast and the remote islands of the St Kilda group.

Passage charts
C66	Mallaig to Rudha Reidh and Outer Hebrides	1:155 000
C67	North Minch and Isle of Lewis	1:155 000
C80	British Isles	1:1 500 000

Imray Digital
ID30   West Britain and Ireland

Rites of Passage   103

Across Biscay

Madeleine Strobel

FALMOUTH TO CAMARIÑAS

We arrived in Falmouth by train on May bank holiday to move back aboard our Bowman 40 *Easy Rider* after her well-deserved re-fit. The clouds were virtually touching the ground. It was bitterly cold and raw in the persistent rain. But the strong to gale force winds in the Bay of Biscay and the English Channel gave us plenty of time to settle back into life aboard and to prepare for our passage. We were embarking double handed across the Bay of Biscay with a tinge of apprehension. Would our crossing be a smooth one or were we going to encounter a rough ride?

Over the coming days we monitored the weather, got up to speed with our brand new electronic charting and multi-function displays, stowed away everything safely for a potentially rough crossing, checked all the systems, and did all the essential last-minute shopping.

Powering up the touch screen of our new navigation system gave an intermittent but persistent low-voltage warning, despite fully charged service batteries. The engineer who fitted the system told us we could ignore this. Trusting his opinion, we did.

We were looking for a suitable weather window. An extensive, deepening low (983mb) west of Spain and an extremely powerful high (1042mb) over Iceland were forecast to drive easterly winds instead of the customary south-westerlies. This was an excellent wind direction for the crossing and the situation was predicted to persist for a while. Fortunately for us, the low was almost stationary and would start filling and then moving slowly west. So, according to the forecasts, we could expect the easterlies to drop right off before a trough associated with the extensive low-pressure system out in the North Atlantic would bring stronger easterlies Force 4-5, occasionally 6 near the coast of Spain. It all sounded positive, particularly the wind direction.

We left Falmouth as the stronger easterlies tailed off in the English Channel. The wind was certainly decreasing as predicted, but the visibility was poor and the sea state still moderate. But that first night and the following day were uneventful. It was a beautiful and smooth reach in Force 3 from the east. We headed south-westwards on about 205°T and by morning we were about 45 miles west of Ushant, into deeper water but not yet off the continental shelf.

We were entertained by the antics of some swallows which kept circling our boat. One of them landed under the spray-hood and nestled in the coiled up halyard. The most intrepid one even decided to enter the galley and stayed overnight.

The wind started to increase at dusk on that second day but steadied at Force 4-5. It was a perfect sail; *Easy Rider* lively and eager and making 6-7 knots through the whole starry night. We marvelled at our new navigation system on which the AIS and the radar could be overlaid. We had never had such sophistication. It really took away some of the anxiety of identifying and tracking the vessels around us.

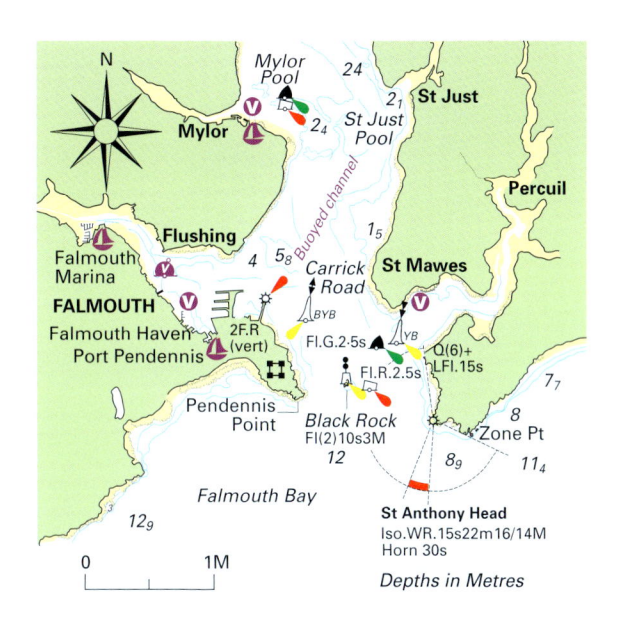

I emerged for my dawn watch with a splitting headache and feeling sick. As we had crossed the edge of the continental shelf the easterly wind had been increasing and clashing with the Atlantic swell, creating a rough and confused wave pattern. Stephan decided to put a second

Opposite
Gale force winds on Day 3 across Biscay
Madeleine Strobel

Below
Leaving Falmouth
Lesley Harry

Rites of Passage 105

13 ACROSS BISCAY

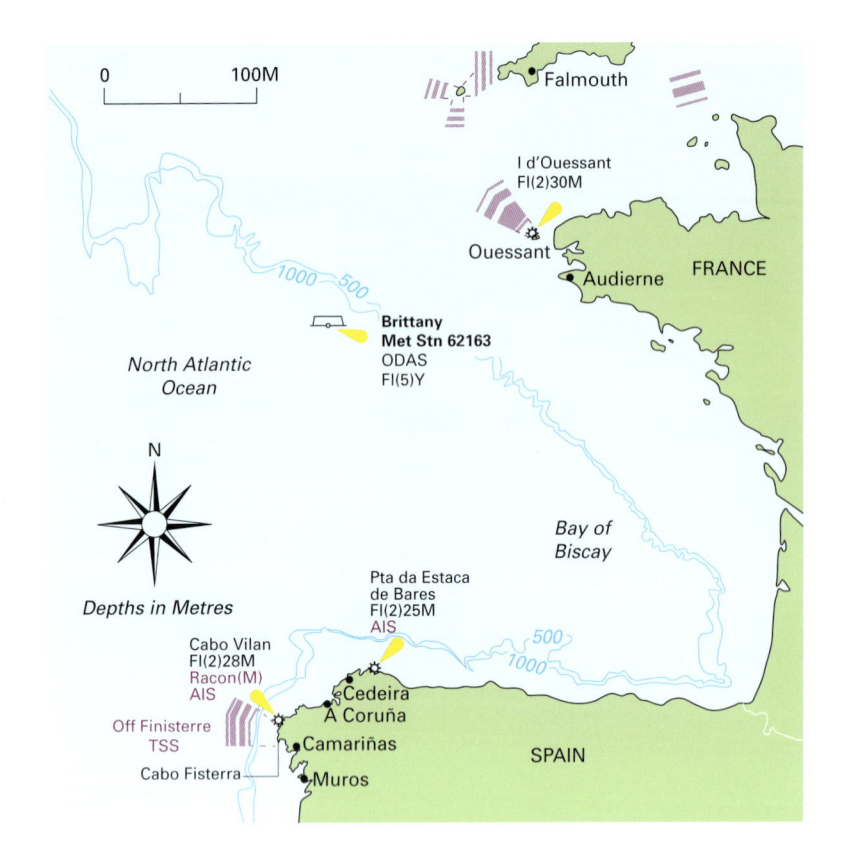

The author seasick at the helm
Stephan Strobel

PASSAGE PLANNER

Leaving from the UK there are several ways to cross Biscay and each of them has its merits. The traditional route involves staying well offshore, sailing outside Ouessant (on approx. 205°T from Falmouth) towards 10°W. This route takes you into deeper water to avoid the worst of the steep seas on the continental shelf should the weather deteriorate. However, once you are this far west, it is difficult to change your mind and seek refuge in Brittany.

A favourable and settled weather forecast is therefore crucial for this strategy, but stable weather can be hard to find in Biscay, which tends to sit on the boundary of high- and low-pressure systems.

An alternative approach is to head across the Channel to Brittany and then day hop around to Audierne. From there to Cedeira is around 300 miles, which significantly reduces both the time at sea and the length of weather window required. It is also perfectly feasible to skirt the whole edge of the bay and daysail nearly all of it. For those with more time and less confidence this is a good way to achieve the same goal. The lovely rias of northwest Spain are a worthwhile reward for the challenge of Biscay.

106 Rites of Passage

reef in before retiring from his watch. But there was a problem with the reefing line, which had been replaced in Falmouth. The new line was thicker and stiffer than the old one and would not run freely. It was a two-person operation to resolve properly, but my seasickness had rendered me absolutely useless, so we hove-to for a few hours so that Stephan could sleep, and I could recover enough to assist. We were then able to put all three reefs in, which was a good thing because by midnight of that third day the wind had reached gale force. We were obviously entering the trough that we were expecting, although we hadn't expected a Force 8!

From our cockpit the waves appeared quite phenomenal, but beautiful in their own right and it was an exhilarating experience as *Easy Rider* continued to reach effortlessly in gusts edging up to Force 9. A school of dolphins joined us for play time, leaping out of our bow wave and circling around for more. Coaming crests burst across our cockpit and creamed over our toe rails and along the coach roof.

During this roller-coaster ride it was hard to see anything beyond the tops of the waves through the spray. Around 60 miles off the coast of Spain, we were approaching the Off Finisterre Traffic Separation Scheme (TSS). Then, suddenly, the wind dropped abruptly within the space of one hour. It was as if someone had turned off the switch. We cleared the TSS under engine and without much traffic.

As it turned out, the calm was just a blip to fool us. The wind veered suddenly to the south and strengthened to the point that we were stopped in our tracks. We had been aiming for Muros, 20 miles south of Cabo Fisterra (Finisterre), but there was no point trying to beat

It was as if someone had turned off the switch
Madeleine Strobel

We had been aiming for Muros in the ría of the same name
Henry Buchanan

13 ACROSS BISCAY

Arrival at Ria de Camariñas

Standard Port A Coruña
HW +0005   LW −0005

MHWS   MHWN   MLWN   MLWS
−1·7m   −1·6m   −0·6m   −0·5m

Entry is feasible day or night, although a first entry by night is not recommended. Keep well clear of Cabo Villano and its offlying rock, El Bufardo, awash at low tide. At night, stay offshore until south of the Las Quebrantas shoal and then come in on the white sector of Punta de Lago light (Oc(2)WRG.6s13m6/4M). The entrance to the ria is fully exposed to the northwest. Seas can mount up in strong winds or seas from this direction. Marina berths are available in Camariñas and at Muxia on the southern side of the ría, or anchor at Camariñas in the shelter of the mole; also S of Cala de Vila, to the N of Camariñas; and to the S of the breakwater at Muxia.

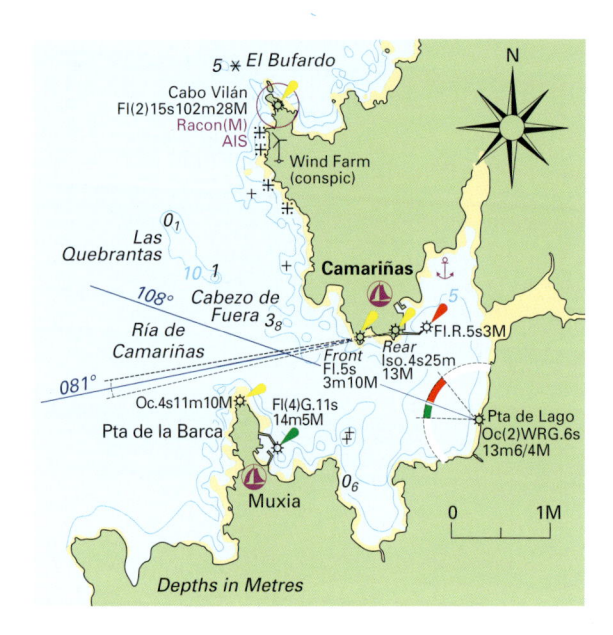

against it, so we bore away to Camariñas, one of the small fishing villages in the Rías Baixas in Galicia, just north of the cape.

We moored up in the marina and after almost 500 miles at sea it wasn't long before we dropped into our bunks. But just as we had fallen into a deep sleep, the Border Control came knocking, wanting to see our passports and ship's papers. They must have been following our progress because they wanted to know why we had suddenly changed course towards Camariñas. Once they had established everything was in order they left as quietly and courteously as they had arrived, and we were free at last to drift off into the deep, contented sleep of a challenge completed.

Camariñas
Madeleine Strobel

WHY CROSS BISCAY?

There are many good reasons to cross Biscay, the first of which are the Rías Baixas. These are a series of flooded valleys, or rias, on the Atlantic coast of Galicia, right in the northwest corner of Spain. This coast is generally wild and rugged, as its name, Costa da Morte, suggests. It is a windswept, treacherous coast exposed to frequent Atlantic gales. But the rias, several of which lie inside a protective chain of islands, open up a completely different world of sheltered waters

108   Rites of Passage

and the warm embrace of Galician culture and hospitality.

From Ría de Vigo it is possible to visit some of the most wonderful wild scenery and unspoilt beaches in Spain. The Cíes Islands, part of the Atlantic Islands National Park, have the most fantastic beach called Praia das Rodas, which has been voted the 'best beach in the world'. During high tide the sea flows in from the Atlantic side of the islands and replenishes a crystal-clear lagoon behind a long dune of soft, snow-white sand. Not surprisingly the Romans called the Cíes 'the islands of the Gods'! You will need a permit to visit this archipelago with your own boat, but it is only a short ferry ride from Vigo itself.

There are many wonderful places to be discovered in Galicia. Santiago de Compostela is one of the highlights and is an easy day trip from the coast. It has always been the culmination of the pilgrimage of the Camino de Santiago. The cathedral itself, home to the relics of St James, is surrounded by grandiose plazas within the mediaeval walls and colonnaded streets of the old town. There are a number of other beautiful towns within the rias and nearby, their ancient stone grain houses a common feature. Many host fiestas which are a vibrant immersion into local food and drink, music, dance and culture.

So, a crossing of Biscay is certainly worthwhile to discover the lovely cruising grounds of Galicia. A direct return trip involves the same considerations of wind and swell as the outward passage. Perhaps more rewarding is a more leisurely cruise along the north coast of Spain and all the way up the French coast. It is possible to go the whole way in day passages if time and conditions allow. A few longer passages will reduce the overall timings.

But another reason for crossing Biscay is to continue onwards, either down the coast of Portugal, towards the Canaries if intending to cross the Atlantic or, as we did, to sail to the Mediterranean. The wind sweeping the northwestern corner of Spain can be very strong. If winds swing south of west near Cabo Fisterra it makes the passing of the cape more laborious. Our track across Biscay, aiming to reach 10°W, the NW corner of the Off Finisterre TSS gave us the advantage of being in a position to round the cape without having to claw our way to windward. If you are heading onwards, 10°W is also a very good position from which to take advantage of the *nortada*, the summer northerlies that blow down the Atlantic coast of Portugal. Though it would be a shame to rush on past the rias which are an ideal place to reward your rite of passage with a more leisurely cruising pace.

Praia das Rodas, Islas Cies, the 'best beach in the world'
Shutterstock Mauricio Graiki

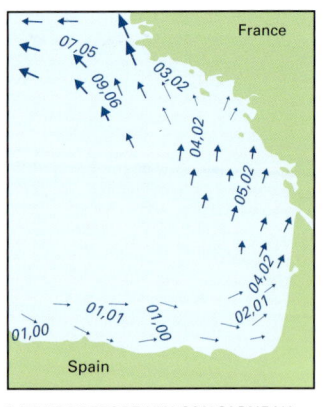

13 ACROSS BISCAY

5 HOURS BEFORE HW CONCARNEAU

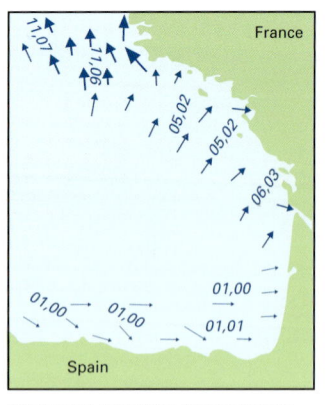

4 HOURS BEFORE HW CONCARNEAU

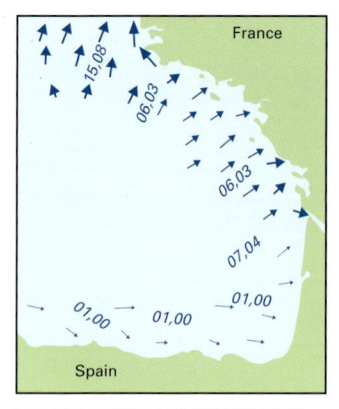

3 HOURS BEFORE HW CONCARNEAU

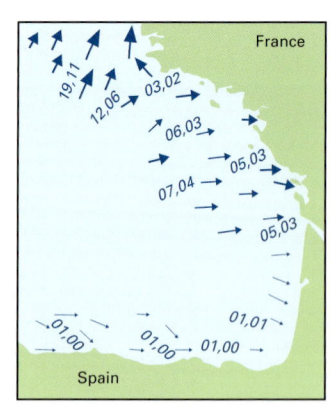

2 HOURS BEFORE HW CONCARNEAU

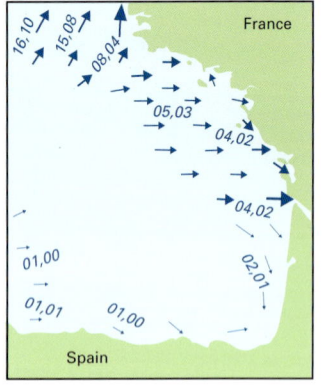

1 HOUR BEFORE HW CONCARNEAU

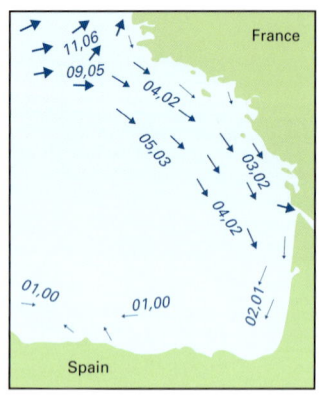

HW CONCARNEAU

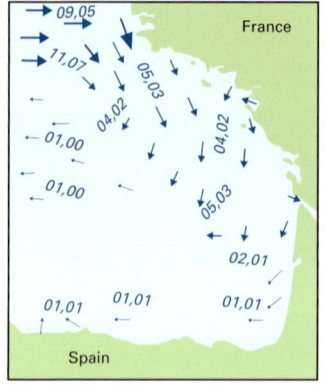

1 HOUR AFTER HW CONCARNEAU

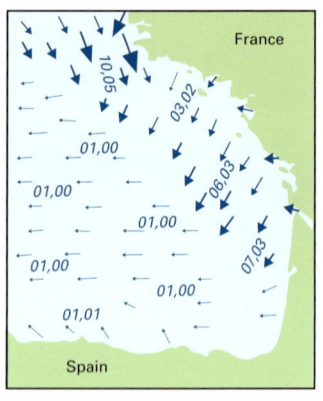

2 HOURS AFTER HW CONCARNEAU

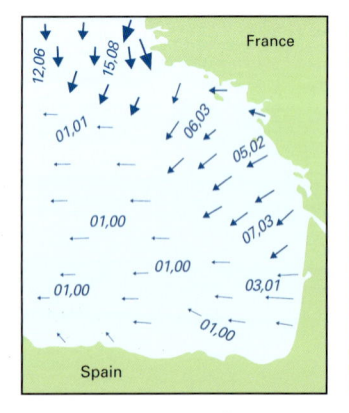

3 HOURS AFTER HW CONCARNEAU

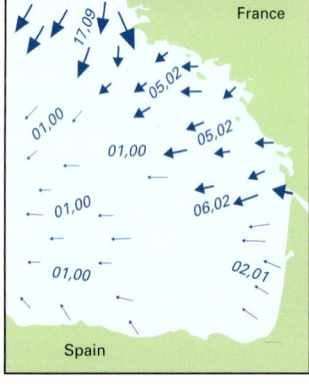

4 HOURS AFTER HW CONCARNEAU

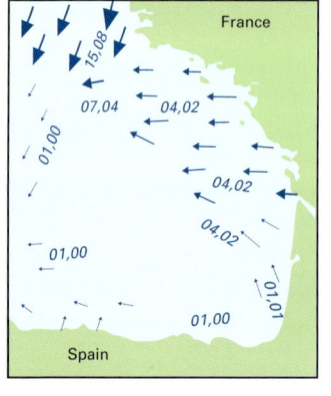

5 HOURS AFTER HW CONCARNEAU

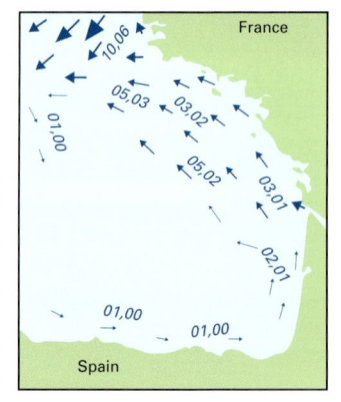

6 HOURS AFTER HW CONCARNEAU

TIDAL STREAMS

The figures shown against the arrows are the mean rates at springs and neaps in tenths of a knot. Thus 15,07 – mean springs rate 1·5 knots, mean neap rate 0·7 knots

IMRAY TIDES PLANNER

Imray Tides Planner app is a useful planning tool. Download from the App Store or Google Play.

110 Rites of Passage

Islote Arenoso, in the
Ría de Arousa
Geraldine Hennigan

About the author

MADELEINE STROBEL's passion for the sea started as soon as she set foot on a sailing boat as a teenager. Along with her husband Stephan and their sons, she has sailed short cruises in the Baltic, Greece and Turkey. They bought their Bowman 40 Easy Rider in 1996 and started cruising further afield, spending eight years sailing around the coasts of Scandinavia, as far as the Gulf of Bothnia, Lake Saimaa and the Lofoten. In 2017, they crossed the Bay of Biscay on their way to the Mediterranean. The couple have also written the Royal Cruising Club Pilotage Foundation's pilot guide to *Corsica and North Sardinia*.

Imray books and charts

Atlantic Spain and Portugal
Henry Buchanan / Royal Cruising Club Pilotage Foundation (Imray)

The classic guide to this varied coast which includes the rias of of Galicia, the estuaries of the Douro and Tejo with Lisbon, the Algarve and then the coast of Andalucia down to Gibraltar. It's the essential companion for yachts making passage to the Mediterranean or onwards to the Canaries before an Atlantic crossing.

Atlantic France
Ouessant to the Spanish Border
Nick Chavasse / Royal Cruising Club Pilotage Foundation (Imray)

The authoritative cruising companion for this long and varied coastline with its sometimes-daunting tides and currents … welcomed both by first-time visitors to the region and by old hands who are revisiting their favourite haunts.

Passage charts

C10	Western English Channel passage chart	1:400,000
C18	Western approaches to English Channel and Bay of Biscay	1:1,000,000
C48	A Coruña to Porto	1:350 000

Imray Digital
ID20 English Channel
ID40 Atlantic France, Iberia and Atlantic Islands

Index

Alderney 49, 50, 51–3
Amsterdam 57, 60–61
Angle Bay 37
Anse des Blancs Sablons 74
Anse de Porsmoguer 74
Ardmore Islands 41–3
Audierne 76, 77, 106

Baie des Trépassés 75
Barra Head 85
Bembridge (IoW) 49–50
Bergen 90, 91–3
Biscay 104–111
Black Deep 26–7
Blackwater river 28
Bolt Head 20
Braye (Alderney) 49, 50, 51–3
Bressay (Shetland) 89, 90
Brest 69, 75, 77
Brightlingsea 28
Bristol Channel 32–9
Brittany 51, 64–79, 106
Brixham 18, 21
Bryher 11, 13
Bull Pt (Rathlin) 43, 44
Burnham-on-Crouch 28

Cala de Vila 108
Camaret 75, 77
Camariñas 108
Cap de la Hague 51, 52
Cape Cornwall 33
Cape Wrath 81, 82–3
Carantec 69
Carrick Roads 9, 65
Cedeira 106
Channel Islands 48–55
Chateaulin 77
Chatham 29
Chavasse, Nick 72–9
Chenal du Four 65, 72–4, 76, 77
Cherbourg Peninsula 51, 52
Chichester Hbr 17
Cíes Islands 109
Clay, Megan 16–23
Cleddau river 36–7
Cooper, Garth 56–63
Corblets Bay (Alderney) 53
Cork Sand 25, 26
Corryvreckan 41, 42
Costa da Morte 108–9
Crinan Canal 41, 42
Crouch river 28
Crow Sound (Scilly) 12
Cumberlidge, Jane 32–9

Dale 36, 37
Dartmouth 21
Deep Water Route 58
Dittisham 21
Douarnenez 75–6, 77
Dover 29

English Channel 48–55, 64–71, 105, 106

Falmouth 9–10, 65, 66, 105, 106
Faux, Ronald 83
Finisterre/Cabo Fisterra 107–8, 109
Fisherman's Gat 26, 27
France 51, 52, 64–79, 105–9

Galicia 108–9
Gibbs, Peter 24–31
Gigha 41
Griffiths, Maurice 29
Gunfleet Sand 25, 26, 28

Hamble river 49, 50
Hardangerfjord 93
Harris 84–5
Hartland Pt 35
Harwich 25, 26, 28, 29, 57, 58
Haverfordwest 36, 37
Heiney, Paul 88–92, 95
Hogbin, Ros 48–55

IJmuiden 57, 58, 59–61
IJsselmeer 61
Inverewe Gardens 84
Ireland (Northern) 41, 42, 43–5
Iroise Sea 73, 74–5
Islay 41
Isle of Wight 49–51

Jura 41, 42

Kean, Norman 40–47
Kentish Knock 26
Kettle's Bottom 33
Kingsbridge 20, 21
Kintyre 41–3, 45
Korsfjorden 91, 92
Kyle of Tongue 82, 83

L'Aber Wrac'h 65–9, 73, 74
L'Aber-Ildut 76
Landguard Pt 57
Land's End 10, 33, 34
Lawrence, Jason 64–71
Le Conquet 74, 76
Lerwick 89–90
Lewis 81, 85, 98
Libenter (L'Aber Wrac'h) 67, 68, 73
Linney Head 34, 35, 36
Lizard Pt 9–10, 66
Llewellyn, Sam 8–15
Loch Eriboll 82
Loch Ewe 84
Loch Inver 83, 84
Loch Roag 98
Loch Tarbert (Harris) 84–5
Lochmaddy 100
Lomax, Judy 93
London Array 26, 27
Long Sand 25, 26, 27
Longis/Longy Bay (Alderney) 49, 53
Longships 10, 33
Lulworth Cove 17, 18
Lundy Island 33, 34–5
Lyme Bay 16–23

McKenzie, Compton 85
Maldon 28
Maplin Sands 28
Marconi, Guglielmo 45
Margate 26, 27, 29
Markermeer 61
Max, Mary 96–103
Medway river 28, 29
Milford Haven 33, 34, 36–7
Mingulay 85
Molène, Ile 73, 76

Morgat 75, 77
Morlaix 69
Mullion 9–10
Muros 107
Muxia 108

Naze Tower 25, 26, 29
Needles (IoW) 49, 50
Netherlands 57–63
New Grimsby (Scilly) 11, 12
Neyland 37
night sailing 57–60, 65–6, 83, 90, 93
Noordzeekanaal 57, 60
North Channel 40–47
North Foreland 25, 26, 27, 29
North Sea 56–63, 88–95
Norway 83, 89, 90–95

Oostende 57
Orkney 81–2
Orwell, George 41
Orwell river 26, 29
Oslofjord 93
Ouessant/Ushant 66, 73, 76, 105, 106
Outer Hebrides 84–5, 96–103

Padstow 33, 34
Paludin 73
Pembroke Dock 37
Penzance 33, 34
Plod Sgeiran 42–3
Ploumanac'h 69
Portland Bill & Race 17, 18, 19
Portsall Inner Passage 73
Portz-Illien 74
Praia das Rodas 109
Pye End 25, 26, 29

Queenborough 29
Quénard Pt (Alderney) 51, 52, 53

Ramsgate 25, 26, 27, 28–9
Rathlin Island 42, 43–5
Raunefjorden 92
Raz de Sein 72, 73, 75–6, 77
Ría de Camariñas 108
Ría de Vigo 109
Rías Baixas 108–9
River Crouch 28
Round Island (Scilly) 11, 12
Runnel Stone 33, 34
Ryfylke (Norway) 93

St Alban's Head 17, 18
St Anne (Alderney) 53
St Anthony Head 65
St Catherine's Pt (IoW) 50, 51
St Govan's Head 36
St Gowan Shoals 34, 35
St Helen's Pool (Scilly) 12
St Ives 33–4
St Kilda 85, 96–103
St Malo 69
St Martin's (Scilly) 11, 12
St Mary's (Scilly) 11, 12
St-Mathieu, Pte de 74, 75
Ste-Evette 76
Salcombe 18, 19–21
Sandy Haven 37
Santiago de Compostela 109

Scarba 41
Scilly 8–15
Scotland 40–43, 80–90, 96–103
Seaport Marina (IJmuiden) 60
seasickness 13, 89–92, 105–7
Seven Stones Reef 10
Sheppey 29
Shetland 89–90
Shiant Is 84–5
Shipwash Channel 57, 58
Skokholm & Skomer 37
Slapton Sands 18–19
Sledway Channel 57, 58
Smalls Cove 20
Sognefjord 93
Solent 49–50
Sound of Harris 85, 98, 100
Sound of Hoy 82
Sound of Jura 41, 42
Southampton Water 49
Spain 106–8
Start Pt 18–19, 20
Stavanger 93
Stewart, Hugh 80–87
Stone Pt (Thames) 25
Stornoway 81, 85
Strobel, Madeleine 104–111
Stromness 81–2
Sunk Sand 25, 26
Sunny Cove 20
The Swinge (Alderney) 51, 52, 53

Taransay 97, 98
Tarbert (Harris) 84, 85
Tayvallich 41
Thames Estuary 24–31
Titchmarsh Marina 25, 29
Tresco (Scilly) 11, 12–13

Ushant/Ouessant 66, 73, 76, 105, 106

Wales 33, 34, 35–9
Walton Backwaters 25, 26, 29
Western Isles 81, 84, 85, 96–103
Western Rocks (Scilly) 13
Whitstable 29
wildlife 13, 29, 37, 42–5, 53, 85, 99–101
wind farms 26, 27, 57, 59, 60
Wolf Rock 10
Woolverstone 57
wrecks & wrecking 13, 29, 34, 45, 73, 76, 85